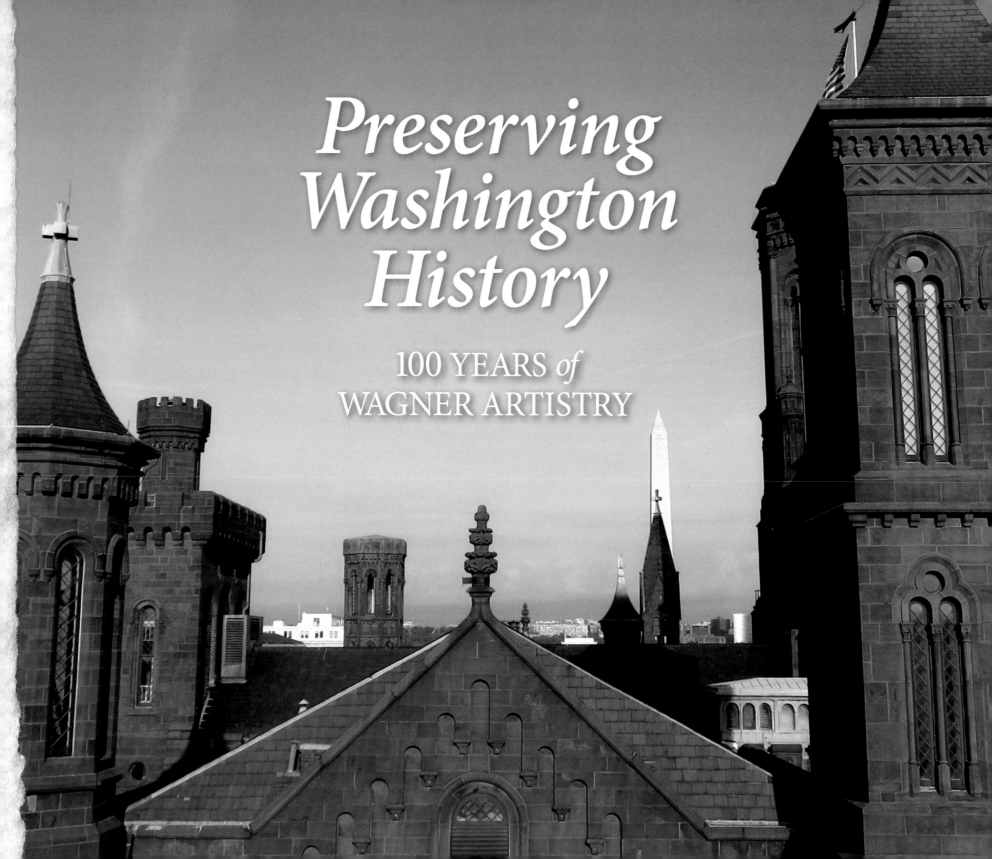

Preserving Washington History

100 YEARS *of* WAGNER ARTISTRY

Preserving Washington History

100 YEARS *of* WAGNER ARTISTRY

**CHUCK WAGNER
AND SHEILA WAGNER**

Foreword by Knight Kiplinger

Hamilton Books
an imprint of
University Press of America,® Inc.
Lanham • Boulder • New York • Plymouth, UK

Published by
Hamilton Books
4501 Forbes Boulevard
Suite 200
Lanham, Maryland 20706

Estover Road
Plymouth PL6 7PY
United Kingdom

ISBN 978-0-7618-6448-6 (hardcover : alk. ppr.)
ISBN 978-0-7618-6449-3 (ebook)

♾™ The paper used in this publication meets the minimum
requirements of American National Standard for Information
Sciences—Permanence of Paper for Printed Library Materials,
ANSI Z39.48—1984

Dedication

It has been 100 years since my grandfather, Otto Wagner, a German immigrant, started Wagner Roofing in 1914 with little more that his tools and a truck. Weathering the Great Depression, he developed a following of loyal customers. In 1937 Otto died and my father, Jack Saunders Wagner, made the decision to take over the business and provide for his mother. He was just 17. The company consisted of a Ford Panel truck and a basement shop. In 1960, my brother, Jack, Jr., at the age of 21, took over the company when our father had health issues. I was able to complete my college education and in 1966 started full time with the company.

I owe much to the family members who came before me. They dedicated themselves to providing for their families and those who worked for them during difficult and trying times. It has been a challenge walking in the footsteps of such men, but they left a legacy of excellence in workmanship and service which continues today.

The photos in this book represent the work performed by our highly skilled crafts-men who have the expertise and pride to complete such challenging projects. We cannot achieve quality without quality workers.

Along the way, our loyal customers have understood and appreciated our work. And we thank them.

And of course, I would like to thank my wife and partner, Sheila Wagner, for her tireless support. Her research, writing and editing made this book possible.

Chuck Wagner

NATIONAL REGISTER OF HISTORIC PLACES

Buildings with this symbol indicate a property designated on the National Register of Historic Places. Sixty-nine of the projects in this book are in this category.

Save America's Treasures is a federal initiative to preserve and protect historic buildings, arts, and published works. It is a public-private partnership between the U.S. National Park Service and the National Trust for Historic Preservation. The National Endowment for the Arts, Heritage Preservation, and the National Park Foundation also are allied.

Table of Contents

Foreword by Knight Kiplinger

There are two equally remarkable things about Wagner Roofing: first, the quality of their work on the most challenging roofs in Washington; and second, their survival as a family-run business for 100 years.

Their work is arguably the most important task in the building trades, because the roof is the soul of a building. A structure cannot be sound and durable without a tight, strong roof. Aesthetically, the roof is literally the crowning touch, the highest and often most visible feature of the structure.

In the Victorian era, roofs became elaborate designs, with varying slopes, materials and decorative elements. And now the great roofs of yesterday — some more than 150 years old — are in dire need of care. That's where Wagner Roofing comes in, climbing to the heights of their profession to make these intricate roofs as strong and handsome as when they were new.

Founded in 1914 by Otto Wagner, the company was a mainstream roofer for most of its corporate life, doing everything from asphalt shingles on tract housing to commercial roofing of all sorts — and doing it all very well, indeed.

But when Chuck Wagner and his wife, Sheila, became the proprietors some 25 years ago, they took this venerable family business in a new direction: the preservation of roofs on the most historic buildings in the national capital region: churches, museums, monuments, man-sions of the Gilded Age, and federal government buildings. Today Wagner roofing is the go-to company for the toughest jobs around, from the Old Post Office to Tudor Place, from Georgetown University to Mahan Hall at the U.S. Naval Academy in Annapolis.

I've known Chuck and Sheila for almost 30 years, when we were all PTA parents together at Horace Mann, our children's elementary school in D.C. As the steward of a family business myself — albeit one that is only 94 years old — I respect the way they have upheld their family's tradition of quality work, customer satisfaction, and respect for the skilled employees who are the heart of their business.

I have experienced their fine work firsthand, as a customer and admirer of their craft. And as a journalist, I enjoy every issue of their lively, informative newsletter, Wagner Rooflines, a model of effective corporate communications. (My 95-year-old father, Austin, is a big fan of it, too.)

It's hard to keep a business in the family for a century, given the vagaries of estate taxes, familial tensions, and the shifting interests of each generation of offspring. But the Wagners have managed to do it and thrive. And our cityscape is richer for it.

Knight Kiplinger is president of Kiplinger Publications in Washington, D.C.

Celebrating 100 Years

Running a successful roofing company is a complicated proposition. Not only must the owner understand roofing, he or she must also understand contract law, labor law and employment law; understand a host of government regulations; be able to manage a diverse workforce; be able to make sales – and then be able to make payroll at the end of every week.

But having a roofing company succeed for 100 years is simply amazing. Not many have managed to survive that long, and those that have often survive only with an assortment of difficulties.

Not so with Wagner Roofing. Chuck Wagner, with the more-than-able help of his wife Sheila, has managed to transform an old-line business into a model enterprise. When most people think of roofs, they think of the thing that keeps water out of their home or building. Wag-ner Roofing looks at roofs in a whole new way: they are works of art, each one unique, each one offering new challenges, each one requiring incredible skill and attention to detail.

Whether it's a roof on the Naval Academy, or the U.S. Capitol, or the Rotunda at the University of Virginia, Wagner's artistry is as obvious as the roof's elegance.

We're proud that Wagner Roofing has been a member of the National Roofing Contractors Association for most of its first 100 years. The company exemplifies what professional roofing contractors are all about, and we fully expect its next hundred years to be just as eventful.

William A. Good
Executive Vice President
National Roofing Contractors Association

Acknowledgments

We want to acknowledge Carol M. Highsmith for contributing images to the Library of Congress for projects including this photo book. Most photos are from Wagner Roofing archives. Chuck Wagner took a majority of the images. And other sources are credited.

Also, we want to thank Ted Landphair for helping us write and tell our story.

Designed and edited by visuallydynamic.com.

Sheila and Chuck Wagner celebrate Wagner Roofing Company's 100th anniversary at the Belmont Mansion. Photo by Chris Zarconi, zarconiphoto.com.

A nod to the past with an eye to the future

A new generation of Wagner Roofing Company leadership looks to the next 10, 20, 30 and 100 years with a keen sense of responsibility for the company's distinction and status in the roofing industry and in the Washington, D.C., community. • Understanding the core fundamentals that have contributed to a successful first 100 years forms the basis for Wagner's trek toward another 100 years as the Washington area's roofing and restoration contractor of choice.

With an ongoing commitment to produce work of the highest standard and to identify, train, and develop the next generation of craftsmen in the field, the company moves into its next century with much the same approach as founder Otto Wagner in 1914.

"We cannot take credit for the entire hundred years," CEO Chuck Wagner says, "but one thing I have tried to live by was to protect my grandfather's and father's great reputations."

Wagner Roofing's reputation and involvement in greater Washington provides a solid foundation and will help the company remain ahead of the curve, not only locally but nationally as a respected elder statesman of the industry.

Dean Jagusch is Wagner Roofing's new president. He has demonstrated a keen sense of the company's distinction in both the roofing industry and in the Washington community, and will assume the responsibility of building on that foundation.

"Moreover, he shares the commitment of my grandfather, Otto, to produce work of the highest standard and cultivating the next generation of craftsmen in the field," Chuck says.

It is exciting to think about what Wagner Roofing will look like a decade or even a quarter-century from now. No one can know. But one thing is for certain: The dedication to producing and standing behind the highest-quality work with the best team in the industry will not waiver.

Otto Wagner and his wife, Anna, in the 1920s.

Above, Jack Wagner Sr., right, circa 1948 with his roofing crew and the '47 Dodge that they called "The Flying Enterprise."

At right, Jack Jr. and Chuck Wagner in 2011.

Wagner Roofing, Since 1914

In 1975, before any and every tidbit of information could be found on the Internet, Chuck Wagner, now CEO of Wagner Roofing, drove from his shop in Hyattsville, Maryland, into Washington, D.C., to the Library of Congress. The National Association of Home Builders had invited him to Chicago to speak about the roofing trade. He figured there might be a historical nugget or a useful insight to be found at the world's greatest collection of human knowledge and creativity.

So, like other researchers in the majestic Main Reading Room of the Thomas Jefferson Building, he put in a request for books that might give him something useful, if not profound.

And it didn't take long to find it. In fact, he stopped at the first sentence: a truism that speaks to roofing's place among crafts.

"The oldest trade: shelter."

Indeed.

Humans have been putting up roofs since they ventured out of caves. Not expertly at first, and not with the artistry or array of materials that Wagner Roofing craftsmen employ today. As the company celebrates its 100th anniversary in 2014, it has achieved high status as roofer to some of the most important institutions, revered places of worship, world-famous museums, and influential individuals in the nation's capital. From an inauspicious start in its founder's basement, the company has risen to the pinnacle of the trade, figuratively and literally, atop such landmarks as the White House, the Washington National Cathedral, D.C.'s towering Old Post Office Building, the Maryland State House, and Tudor Place in Georgetown.

"Washington, D.C., is a unique city in which to run a roofing business," Chuck wrote in 2003 in the company newsletter, Rooflines, "especially if you enjoy architecture and the quality of buildings on which we are privileged to work. Our interest in old buildings is complemented by our employees' ability to re-create a roof equal to or better than the existing one."

And the job is rarely easy. Chuck's brother, Jack Jr., who operated the company from 1960 to 1991 with Chuck, calls roofing "mining in the sky." It deals with many of the same materials as mining: copper, tin, slate, ladders, ropes, and pulleys. It's grueling work — and it was twice as hard in the days before sturdy scaffolding, hoists and cranes, computer sheet-metal fabrication, and computer imagery.

It's beastly hot work, too, come summertime in Washington. One day in 2010, for instance, when Wagner crews were installing a new copper dome and the Star of David atop the historic synagogue at Sixth and I streets NW, the temperature reflecting off the 4.2 tons of copper hit 120 degrees — at 8:30 in the morning!

And roofing can be brutally cold work with the arrival of the biting winds of winter. It is then or during a spring deluge, that the company phone rings and rings as people frantically call for help. A roofer's ladder against a house is a most welcome sight when wet, thigh-high snows press up to 56 pounds of pressure per cubic foot on old roofs, ice dams in gutters back snowmelt under shingles and into living rooms, or steady rain finds a low point right where a seam has opened.

Roofing is dangerous, despite precautions and incessant scrutiny from federal, local, and — in Wagner Roofing's case — the company's own safety watchdogs. A 2011 CNN Money ranking of America's most dangerous jobs placed roofing sixth. Roofers must deal with steep inclines, slick dew and frost, and sudden cloudbursts.

Today, everyone's tied off in harnesses, secured to the structure, or to a scaffold. "There's no freelancing up there like the old days," Chuck says.

The company's crew chiefs keep their eyes on two things at all times: their men and the sky. Supervisors rely on the Weather Channel and satellite reports to keep crews updated on outside conditions.

They'll tell you roofing's not a job for the faint of heart, acrophobes, or those prone to vertigo. "I was never afraid of heights," jokes Jack Jr. "I was afraid of falling."

J.S. Wagner Company operated from 2024 Rhode Island Avenue NE, from 1951 to 1968.

Wagner Roofing, with 55 employees, has helped elevate the roofing trade in public esteem and has been entrusted with delicate renovations or overhauls for such entities such as the 6th & I Historic Synagogue, the Department of Justice's main building, and the U.S. Naval Academy.

Sheila Wagner, Chuck's wife and the company's vice president, recalls interviewing a young woman for an accounting vacancy.

As the conversation wrapped up, Sheila asked the applicant if she had any questions.

"Yes," the young woman said. "What's a nice couple like you doing in the roofing business?"

Evelyn Wagner in 1949.

Jack Kay, right, discusses with Jack S. Wagner, roofing applicator, details of a new roof covered with CertainTeed Thick Butt Asphalt Shingles at his Connecticut Avenue Estates project in Wheaton, Maryland.

From basement to pinnacle

In Wagner Roofing's case, it runs in the family, going back to 1914, when Chuck and Jack Jr.'s grandfather Otto — a German immigrant and tinsmith — started the company in a metal shop in the basement of a home he built on Evarts Street NE in Washington, D.C. Lacking even a truck in which to carry his tinwork, he once lugged his materials in one hand and his ladder in the other, somehow boarded a streetcar, and then clutched the ladder alongside the car as it clattered to his destination.

Chuck and Jack Jr.'s father, Jack Sr., learned not just his trade but also the value of hard work and integrity from his old man: Otto was a hard-driving taskmaster whom his workers — once he could afford to hire any — called "the Mad Dutchman." Jack Sr. cut tin and "bent metal," as they say in the trade, in his father's shop and even hoisted his father onto jobsites when Otto weakened from his battle with stomach cancer. "Dad would fall asleep on his feet" at the end of an exhausting day, Jack Jr. says.

Otto began his work in the early 20th century in what was then called the roofing and tinning trade under the watchful eye of the Gichner family, who operated Gichner

Sheet Metal for many years. The Gichners preferred to hire German immigrants who brought stellar work habits with them from the Old Country, and they took a liking to Otto.

In those days, the trades did not mix: Tinners did tin roofs and tin roofs alone.

Jack Sr. had left the company and was working at the Government Printing Office — and was ready to accept the track scholarship that American University had offered — when Otto died in 1937. Reluctantly, and mostly to help his mother, Anna, Jack Sr. gave up his government job and that scholarship to take over the business at age 17.

"Bud," he told Jack Jr. years later, "it was a means to an end."

Eventually he had a small but hardy crew of five men and a '47 Dodge panel truck they called the "Flying Enterprise." He treasured those men. "You get good men, everything else follows," he says. They kept him going through the hard times.

Jack Sr. moved the company's operations to larger and nicer quarters on Rhode Island Avenue NE and set up a shop in the basement and the office upstairs. He kept his parents' property on Evarts Street, though, as a truck and supply yard.

His parents' old house, which was covered with shingles of seven colors, became a source from which to scavenge weathered shingles for Wagner insurance jobs, when color matches were critical.

The expanding company would move operations one more time, in 1969, to Hyattsville, across the Maryland line in Prince George's County, from which Wagner trucks roll to this day.

In the early 1940s, Jack Sr.'s role in the company was interrupted. He was in the Army, off in Europe — working on a tile roof in occupied Italy. His wife, Evelyn, held down the fort back home.

"You couldn't buy trucks or cars, it being wartime," she told her son Chuck one day. "I had a four-door '36 Ford they put ladder racks on it and sometimes remembered to take them off at night. Many a night, my girlfriends and I went out with 40-foot ladders on the car."

Evelyn and Jack Sr. wrote letters. In one, Evelyn brought her husband up to date on company affairs:

The firm of Wagner and Wagner have 2 new customers, I'll have you know. They came from the ad in the [Washington] Star, which I'm enclosing. You know it dawned on me after I'd sealed the letter last night that the C Street job I was telling you about I forgot to mention the price. The reason I forgot is I finished the letter then figured the job and meant to put the price back in . . . so it's $39.00.

The two new customers are a Mr. Rogers and Mrs. Cowan. Both live in Chevy Chase and have small leaks. No job too small, that's our motto!

Evelyn's tenure and eye for figures produced good family folklore. "Evelyn would round up the bills for Wagner services to the nearest dollar," Chuck says. A $43.50 charge became $44.

"When Jack returned, the customers greeted him with, 'Thank God you're back. We couldn't stand Evelyn's high prices much longer.' "

Like thousands of GIs, Jack Sr. returned to boom times, when cities like the District of Columbia satisfied young Americans' thirst for homeownership and a piece of the American dream as houses sprang up throughout suburbia.

Sleepy Washington was expanding fast, first inside its own borders as homes and businesses spread north, up Georgia Avenue and beyond Rhode Island Avenue in Northeast. Then into the close-in "streetcar suburbs," where a Washington legend, builder Jack Kay, took a liking to Jack Sr. Kay put the Wagner crew to work creating Wheaton, north of Silver Spring, Maryland.

A March 1955 ad for CertainTeed shingles in Practical Building magazine shows Kay and Jack Sr. looking over construction in Wheaton's Connecticut Avenue Estates. The ad says that in eight years, more than 1,200 homes were built, all "roofed by J.S. Wagner" with CertainTeed products.

Jack Jr. and his father in 1945.

Sheila Wagner demonstrates a slate repair at the annual Festival of the Building Arts at the National Building Museum.

"Dad was a gentleman among roofers," Jack Jr. recalls. "He was honest, refused to play games with insurance claims. If he went up on a roof and found only $50 in damage, that's what he'd charge.

"The best testament to his reputation: One company actually put a spy in our shop to find out how we got all the insurance work."

Chuck says his father was admired and liked by the men and customers alike: "There was always a lot of talk around the dinner table about roofing. My brother and I worked at the roofing company during the summers growing up. He took us out with Ray Saffel, one of those wizened mechanics, and he said, 'You take care of these boys.' We learned by watching and by doing."

Beauty meets practicality

To the Wagners, roofs are art forms. "Landscape architects create greenery that's beauty to behold," Jack Jr. says. "Wagner Roofing creates roofscapes with all the materials made by man." Looking at an elegant mansard roof, or an intricate "valley" between a sloping roof and a protruding dormer window where slates have been meticulously laid to create subtle designs, or an enormous copper dome gleaming in the distance, who can argue with him?

Wagner Roofing made its reputation at monumental, historic, and sacred places. But like any roofer, the company wouldn't be in business if it couldn't find and stop the simplest of leaks. It's simple to roofers but a potential disaster to a homeowner or a curator of irreplaceable treasures for whom buckets catching raindrops in the gallery just won't do.

There's more to locating the source of a leak than you might imagine. The principles sound basic: Water takes the path of least resistance to the ceiling above your favorite sofa. But that path may be circuitous and hard to trace beneath a massive roof. It takes a detective's eye, Chuck says, and a lot of experience with water's insidi-

ous capillary action to spot the source.

"A lot of times, it's old-fashioned common sense and deductive reasoning," he says.

The Wagners tell of a big industrial job that they completed in Northeast Washington. Within months, the owner called, barking that the roof was leaking everywhere. "You'll find the problem and fix it, or you'll be putting on a new roof," he shouted.

Jack Jr. drove over to see what could be done, taking along Morris Jones, his sage "mountain man."

"Morris just had an affinity for fixing roofs," Jack Jr. says. "I'm feeling defenseless if the owner and this fellow he called his 'roofing consultant' were right. I'm talking to this consultant, and he's smelling blood. The roof's a block long, and Morris is way over on the other side.

"Just as the guy is saying, 'So when do we get our new roof?' Morris comes over and says, 'This isn't our fault. Stay here for a minute. Should be comin' along in a minute.'

" 'What was he talking about?' I wondered.

"And then — here comes a train! And the building rattles, right under our feet. Morris calmly says, 'We need an expansion joint up here.' " Building movement had caused the leaks, and Jones's deduction saved Wagner Roofing several hundred thousand dollars.

A sign prominent in the Wagner Roofing shop says, "We Take Care of Complaints First." As Chuck puts it: "The first thing you do after a rain is take care of any complaint. You go back to those jobs first."

There has long been a truism in the roofing business: "What we need is a good storm."

And the Washington area got a string of them: Hurricanes Carol, Hazel, Connie, and Diane. In 1954, Hazel produced the 20th century's widest swath of hurricane-force winds and sustained readings of 100 miles per hour right through the normally tranquil capital. Never in memory had the city seen such weather — or such a frantic, stressful, and financially fruitful stretch of work for roofers.

A tile replacement job at Prospect Hill Cemetery Gatehouse (1927) at 2201 North Capitol Street NE.

Bob Wooldridge demonstrates his slate skills at the Festival of the Building Arts at the National Building Museum.

All in the family

But Jack Sr. would have less and less of a part in it. He had a bad heart. He'd still estimate work and show up at jobs and the shop. "Want to keep my hand in," he told the men.

Then Jack Jr. became the new boss in 1960 at age 21. His first job working for his father had been making cleats — the metal that holds down tin roofing — and the sleeves for gutter spikes called ferrules.

"Dad would pay me a penny apiece," Jack Jr. remembers. "I had to fill a keg. But it was more fun just messing around in the shop with the men."

In the 1970s, Hechinger, the Washington area's hardware behemoth in the days before Home Depot and Lowe's, decided to go into the home-improvement business, and it hired Wagner for much of its roofing work.

Chuck took over the company from his brother in 1991, along with the support and partnership of his wife, Sheila. She worked jobs from receptionist to office manager and is co-owner today.

They began to forge a picture of Wagner Roofing that changed the way the company was viewed. Chuck's interest blossomed in architecture and the history of the buildings that the company worked on. Chuck and Sheila began producing Wagner Rooflines, a quarterly publication to highlight recent jobs. They also began to tackle more complex projects.

All in the family: Rachel Wagner followed in the footsteps of her father, grandfather, and great-grandfather by offering her services on the repair of one of Washington's architecturally significant buildings. It's just that this one was only six inches tall. The architectural model of the Kreeger Museum, built by Philip Johnson in 1967, had been kept in storage and was found in poor condition. The model has been repaired and cleaned, and is used for docent training, architectural classes, and children's school tours. Rachel has interned at Clark Construction and Torti Gallas & Partners, an architecture firm in Silver Spring, Maryland. Rachel earned her MS in architecture at Catholic University and currently works as an architect for Gensler.

"We still had my father's good name, but the economy was in a downswing in the '90s. We kept the company going and changed our focus to preservation and restoration," Chuck says. "As Sheila once said, 'With restoration work, your job is never done.'"

In 2005, Rachel Wagner followed in the footsteps of her father, Chuck, by offering her services on the repair of one of Washington's architecturally significant buildings. It's just that this one was only six inches tall. The architectural model of the Kreeger Museum, built by Philip Johnson in 1967, had been kept in storage and was in poor condition. Rachel, great-granddaughter of the company's founder, carries on the family legacy of improving buildings. The repaired Kreeger model is used for docent training, architectural classes, and school tours.

The spirit of Wagner Roofing

Chuck says that when his crews first arrive at a job — even before they meet the homeowner or building proprietor — they "have a huddle." The crew boss opens a file from the estimator explaining what the conditions are, where they should set up, and what the job entails.

But before they even touch a ladder, they go over a checklist of safety reminders, and they sign off that they've read and understood them — every man on the crew, the crew boss included, every time.

"And then we have an independent safety company that we've hired go by about 10 jobs a week," Chuck says. "They send in reports on what they see on a daily basis by e-mail."

Occupational Safety and Health Administration inspectors can appear without notice, prepared to cite violations — the fines for which can mount in $25,000 increments. OSHA can also shut down a worksite or egregiously unsafe company.

What about hazards such as wasps' and hornets' nests? One mechanic recalls a job in Germantown, Maryland, in which a cavity of studded walls was a giant beehive.

That's why Wagner roofers' extensive first-aid kit includes a bee-sting packet.

Before a recent holiday party, "we had our safety company come in and review our safety record for the year. Our system is working. . . . There were no accidents that year," Sheila says. The company handed out awards for best job of the year, safest job, and safest person.

In terms of workplace culture, Chuck says, "ours is a safety culture. I've been through courses myself, talked with our safety people, but I keep hammering it home. Yeah, I guess you'd say we're extreme about it."

And that wasn't all. Sheila reviewed the company's retirement plans, health program — now one of the best in the industry — and drug and alcohol policy. "It's simple, and everybody knows it," she says. "We drug test before hiring and test for alcohol or drugs any time there's an accident. You can't talk all about safety and not be serious about working sober and drug-free."

With an eye to short- and long-term weather forecasts, Chuck draws daily and monthly schedules that include a "rain plan." The long-term one can be sheer guesswork when the weather turns volatile. But the company can make good use of a rain day inside the shop as crews work fabricating gutters and cornices, making skylights, learning soldering techniques, and loading trucks for the next day.

The Wagners also have detailed the accomplishments of many interns that the company has brought aboard, including one — Lee Simon of Hartford, Connecticut, a young fellow from a roofing family — who helped the company's estimators select and install estimating software. In a note of appreciation to them all in 2004, Sheila wrote, "We would like to thank all of these smart young people who have passed through our office and who keep renewing our spirits."

The company's owners may be, in Jack Jr.'s words, "the maestro in the pit." But success in the roofing trade really does come down to the skill of its mechanics and roofers, its shop foremen and estimators, its accountants, its dispatcher, and its collection staff. You're only as good as

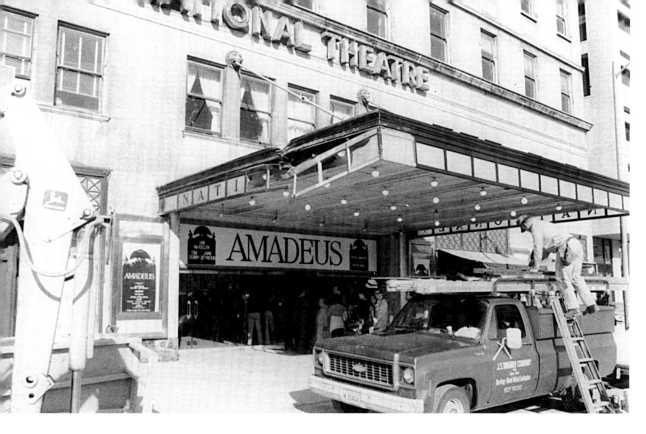

NATIONAL THEATRE (1923)
Architects: Eggers and Higgins. 1321 Pennsylvania Avenue NW. Kenny "Doctor" Howell, Wagner master sheet metal mechanic for 25 years, preps for metal marquee and glass restoration.

your last roof, and customers will call their friends when that last roof was a great one.

As far back as 1997, Chuck noted in the company newsletter that "skilled craftsmen are getting harder to find." Many industries face this problem, he noted, as the labor force changes from an age-old apprenticeship tradition to an "easy-route" workforce. Workers "just aren't as interested in long apprenticeships, in putting in the kind of hard work necessary to learn difficult skills like sheet-metal work. . . . This learning period usually meant a long term of low pay and hard work, a sacrifice most workers today are unwilling and often unable to make."

Nevertheless, Wagner Roofing sets the bar higher than ever. Not just solid experience and demonstrated skill are required to make the grade. Intangibles are critical: curiosity, a desire to learn, a perfectionist's mind-set, maybe even a touch of artistry.

Unique mementoes

There's room for fun at Wagner in moments of camaraderie on the road or in the shop. If there's time on a rainy day, for instance, the staff and the Wagners themselves will get busy on birdhouses. The structures are fashioned from salvaged shakes, metal roofing, and shingles and slates, and they often are given to customers as a token of the company's appreciation.

In one case, tin removed from the roof of Brickyard Hill House (c. 1800) in Georgetown was used to roof both an

antique dollhouse and several birdhouses — collectibles designed by Sheila. Another time, the pastor of St. Paul's Rock Creek was so delighted with her birdhouse that she took it to services and used it as a prop for a sermon on the inner soul.

Many people in Washington now own Wagner-made birdhouses crafted with materials from the National Cathedral, the Belmont Mansion, and the Smithsonian Castle.

When Wagner Roofing reached 90 years in business in 2004, Sheila explained the challenges of a family business in an issue of Rooflines: "It takes a lot of energy to keep up with this ever-changing world. I believe running a company is very much like being a parent: The job does not end."

Chuck says the company's future is in good hands: those of his craftsmen. "We feel a great responsibility to past and future generations of Wagners to maintain excellence in the industry and to putting customers first," he says. "It isn't just our business. It's our good name."

Valuing mechanics and safety

When you ask Jack Jr. about a favorite job or a favorite memory from his three decades in the business, he replies: "What I carry to this day is an appreciation for the mechanics — their skill and determination to get things right. And for their amazing feel for architecture."

When a roofer speaks of "mechanics," he's not talking about someone who fixes boilers or diesel engines or cars. It's a term for a roofing crew's lead man, a jack-of-all-trades journeyman who can craft anything and can size up a problem — in the roof, its underpinning, or a chimney or turret or steeple — and fix it.

Morris Jones's brother, Early, worked for the company for 50 years. Shortly after he signed on in 1950, he was off to Wheaton, Maryland, where, he estimated, "I'll bet we put 1,000 roofs on houses" for Jack Kay.

One day in 1975, Jones and his crew had a memorable

experience with a built-up roof, which happened to be atop the West Wing of the White House.

The Wagner newsletter set the scene in a 1995 story:

The Nixon Administration certainly had its share of leaks to the press. But one leak you may not have heard about occurred in the White House press room 20 years ago. Wagner Roofing Company was called in to repair a roof that was leaking into the press area. For a time, GSA, the building manager, was able to conceal the leak with a copper pan in the ceiling. But the work needed to be done properly, and Wagner Roofing got the job.

Interestingly, we were asked to do the repairs quietly, on the weekend, when the press was not around, with the hope that reporters wouldn't make a story out of it.

Enter Early Jones and his crew. For the job, they had to melt a block of tar, then heat it to 450 degrees, an essential but time-consuming process. The problem was, the security guard assigned to watch them took two daily breaks. "Each time he left," Jones said, "we had to turn off the gas under the kettle, shut down operations, secure the area, and go with him to the Old Executive Office Building" — which was the secure area for contractors.

Such are the twists in a roofer's day.

Jones's grandmother gave him his unusual first name. "But," he says, "I've been on some jobs early in the morning, and the guys say, 'They named you right.' "

Then there was Israel Shimberg, a Russian immigrant who, Jack Jr. says, "was our metal man extraordinaire," about whom there are enough stories to fill a separate book.

"He could make anything in metal," Chuck says. "If he had not fabricated it before, he would figure out a way."

Consider Jack Jr.'s story about Shimberg, who died in 1995:

The shop had made a downspout for the Old Executive Office Building, next to the White House. But I had underestimated just how high the gutter was from the ground. Israel and Herbie Balden took a 60-foot ladder

to check out what had to be done up there, and they came back and said they couldn't reach the roof. It was higher than 60 feet. Well, 60 feet was the tallest ladder we had or could put against a building.

That was bad enough, but we had to get the job done the next day, no question. The Japanese prime minister was coming to town, and they wanted the work done before he got there.

Israel says, "We'll use a boatswain's chair."

Well, we didn't have any boatswain's chairs lying around, let alone a wire-reinforced rope strong enough to hoist one up.

Israel says, "I'll make the chair. Get me a one-inch rope with a quarter-inch cable inside." I called around, couldn't find one.

So he says, "All right, I'll do that myself." He takes this rope, ties it around a stanchion, takes a cable — his body's obscuring what he's doing — and puts it into the folds of the rope. Does it in 15 minutes. And then he makes the boatswain's chair out of a four-inch locust post.

"Some people say that slate work is a lost art due to the lack of quality craftsmen," says Wagner's project superintendent on a re-roofing of Georgetown University's majestic Healy Hall in 2008. "Fortunately, we not only have quality craftsmen, we have Bob. He has probably forgotten more about slate than most of us will ever know."

Bob Wooldridge, 74, is a master mechanic. Fifty-five years into his roofing career, he drives to the jobsite each morning from his home in rural Pennsylvania.

"I like where I live," Wooldridge says. "It's a good-sized farm." And it's a place whose back 40 he's been known to mow upon arriving home after a taxing day on the roofs of Washington.

If Wagner Roofing encounters a unique pattern or cut of slate, perhaps an old one into which a design has been etched — and a match is needed — Wooldridge is the

This birdhouse's tin roof is from Georgetown's Brickyard Hill House, originally occupied by the Peter family in 1914. The house is now the fire control building at the Ritz-Carlton Hotel in Georgetown. The wood base is from a 100-year-old barn.

Bob Wooldridge works on Healy Hall at Georgetown University.

man to see. "Roofers are a lot like farmers," Chuck says, admiringly. "They improvise."

If the workers need training in how to take off tile for a relay job, number it, and put it back exactly where it came from, Wooldridge is called. If a complicated cornice needs to be cut, a fancy window needs to be made, or a painter needs instructions, Wooldridge does the cutting, the making, and the instructing.

"He's a one-man general contractor," Chuck says. "I've seen Bob take a hair dryer to a snow-packed, ice-covered roof that no one else would go near. Or hook a hose to hot water in the bathroom to run out onto the roof and melt the ice. When others go by the book, he gets creative. Whatever it takes to get the job done."

Wooldridge remembers "when we didn't even put up scaffolds. We'd put up two ladders. Fella on one ladder would do the nailing or whatever, and the fella on the other would bring up as much material as he could. When the eaves were set, they'd set the slate on a bracket on the roof and get started up there."

The hardest part of the job? "Fightin' the wind all day on a really windy day. It plays havoc with you. Your legs just ache at the end of the day."

And the weather? (It was he who experienced the 120-degree morning atop the downtown synagogue.) "We can work through cold," Wooldridge says, "but when it starts sleeting . . . boy!"

"I remember once," Wooldridge continues, "we were working up on Foundry United Methodist Church on 16th Street. It was a cold fall day, and there was a prediction of sleet and snow. So we had our eye on the sky, believe you me. But when it came, it hit so fast, and things got so icy right away, that we had to get ropes to get down off the roof."

Once a roof is removed, Wooldridge's crew spends the last minutes of the workday covering the building with roofing felt. Otherwise, as they say in the roofing business, you've bought an interior. Wooldridge received the

Craftsmanship Award from Baltimore's Building Congress and Exchange in 1997 for work on the Gallagher Mansion, which was placed on the National Register of Historic Places in 1983. He was a finalist in the National Roofing Contractors Association for Most Valuable Player in 2001.

"I had a fella, Harold Hargate, broke me in," Wooldridge says. "Nastiest old person I ever worked with. But he was a master at getting things started right. He had a saying that we still use here at Wagner Roofing — made a placard of it that we put up in the shop. The saying is, 'Well begun is half done.' And that applies to everything. If you get the first thing — the scaffold — right, it makes the rest so much easier."

But the most enjoyable part of the job, he says, is coming down, walking around the project, and looking for anything that needs fixing.

"These guys here," he says, pointing to a small crew of Salvadoran Americans working with him on a Wagner tile job atop a caretaker's cottage at Prospect Hill Cemetery off North Capitol Street NE in Washington. "When they're done, they'll go around that whole building. They've got cellphones with cameras, and when I see them take pictures, that's a lot of satisfaction 'cause they're proud of their work and want to show their friends what they did."

Wagner Roofing mechanics' expertise is on display not just on the roofs of Washington. The company has regularly appeared at the Festival of the Building Arts at the National Building Museum, where, each year, 1,000 people or more have watched Wagner Roofing's master craftsmen demonstrate slate and copper roofing techniques. In 2001, they did likewise at the "Masters of the Building Arts" exhibit at the Smithsonian Folklife Festival on the Mall.

And in 2006, the entire nation got a Wagner Roofing demonstration when "This Old House," America's foremost home-improvement television series, followed Tony Cosentino and his Wagner crew as they put a synthetic-slate roof on a house belonging to a low-in-

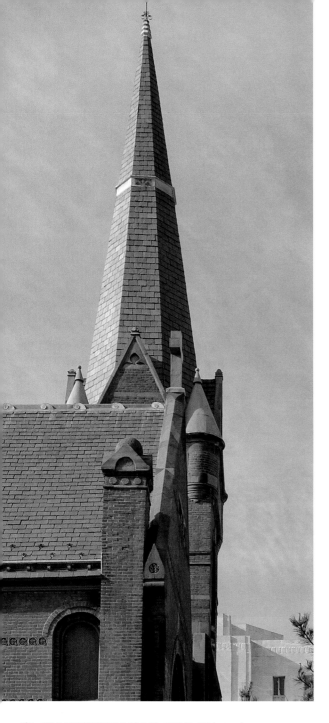

come family at Fifth Street and Massachusetts Avenue NW. Wagner Roofing donated the work to Mi Casa, a nonprofit organization that helps provide housing for underprivileged D.C. residents.

The world of restoration

Two developments propelled Wagner Roofing into the field of historic restoration, for which it is now best known.

"We got the Minkoff account," Chuck says. Minkoff is a huge company, based in Beltsville, Maryland, that specializes in post-disaster restorations — especially after fires. Working as a subcontractor, Wagner Roofing crews began being dispatched to what remained of some of the most complex, beautiful, and expensive roofs in the Washington area.

And the second development that added historic restoration to the Wagner Roofing portfolio?

Churches, says Chuck, starting with St. Mark's at Third and A streets SE in 1974. The company re-roofed the building and salvaged the slates, which the church sold to raise money to help pay for the job. "Salvaging slate, tile, and metal from our projects is a passion with me," Chuck wrote later. "It is interesting to find a [new] place for these historic pieces."

Wagner Roofing has worked on more than 100 church projects, the Washington National Cathedral among them. There have been so many houses of worship, Chuck says with a chuckle, "that people started calling me 'Church Chuck.'"

Pretty soon those jobs led to even bigger ones. Each presented significant challenges. Wagner Roofing tackled them with enthusiasm and soon became known as the roofers who solve problems.

"This Old House," America's foremost home-improvement television series, followed Tony Cosentino and his Wagner crew as they put a synthetic-slate roof on a house in Washington. Mi Casa is the organization that purchased the house, which was renovated and given to a low- income family. Wagner Roofing donated its work on the house.

ST. MARK'S EPISCOPAL CHURCH (1894)
Architects: T. Buckler Ghequier and Delos Smith. 301 A Street SE. Project Architect: George Hartman.

One of 13 restored dormers.

Wagner Artistry

🏛 **U.S. NAVAL ACADEMY MAHAN HALL (1907)**
Architect: Ernest Flagg. Decatur and Maryland Avenues, Annapolis, Maryland. Wagner replaced over 12,000 square feet of slate, 9,000 square feet of copper roofing, and all built-in gutters, fascia, and cornice. Project Architect: Randy Ghertler.

Crews load a restored copper dormer onto a scaffold and then onto the mansard.

U.S. Naval Academy's Mahan Hall

When you ask Chuck Wagner to name his favorite building, his favorite project in the couple of decades that he was in charge, and he'll say, "The next interesting one." But he admits there is a standout: the U.S. Naval Academy's Mahan Hall, which presented real challenges.

"A lot of complex metal work," Wagner says. "Slate roof, built-in gutter, concrete deck. We had to take circular glass — historic glass — very carefully out of 13 dormers. The dormers had been damaged by snow, and we had to remove many dents. It was like doing auto-body work on a vintage car."

Access to the roof required scaffolding that had to be hung or suspended from the flat roof above the radiused slate roof. Specs called for attaching slate to nailers that had been set in concrete many years ago. There were no nailers, so two-by-fours were drilled and screwed into the concrete to create a nailing surface. The flat roof was a rubber surface, which was replaced with 20-ounce copper that was installed using 300 18-by-24 flat-seam pans.

Clockwise starting at upper right: Finished copper bells; finished cheneau on the fascia of the built-in gutter on the slate mansard; patterns for the 12 bells and 26 cheneau being fabricated in Wagner shop; "before" and "after" as wall art in the Wagner company office.

Belmont Mansion

Built for Perry Belmont, a U.S. congressman and grandson of Commodore Matthew Perry, the spectacular, trapezoidal residence (1909) on New Hampshire Avenue in Washington is now the world headquarters of the General Grand Chapter of the Order of the Eastern Star, an organization affiliated with Freemasonry.

The mansion features two ornate circular skylights — one over the Grand Staircase, the other in the Grand Ballroom. When leaks threatened the integrity of the structure and the mansion's priceless artifacts in 2000, Wagner Roofing's father-son team, Randy Herald and Randy Jr., were called in. The scope to replace the two 40-foot-by-40-foot hip-roofed skylight over the staircase included netting the 10-foot shaft below the skylight in the event that anything fell during repairs. Although the valuable torchieres and other furnishings would be moved, the marble floor, brass stair railing, and irreplaceable glass transom had to be protected.

The actual work was undefined until the Wagner team removed the copper caps that hold the glass and the glass itself. "I was surprised to find the glass anchored by three-inch rope," Randy Herald recalls. "We removed all of the original rope, which had disintegrated over the years." He fabricated new copper caps and gutter, cleaned the steel frame and glass, then reinstalled the glass and caps.

Next, Bill Briggs, husband of then-Rightworthy Grand Secretary Betty Briggs, and Chuck Wagner worked to identify the source of leaks in the State Dining Room. They found that some of the 28 copper dormers — roofed structures containing the windows that project through the sloping mansard roof — had holes. Budgeting the mansion's restoration funds required repairing or replacing the dormers in stages, six at a time. "Randy selected priority dormers for repair or replacement according to their degree of deterioration," Briggs explains.

So far, Herald has repaired a dozen dormers and is scheduled to work on six more. Briggs seems especially pleased that, thanks to Wagner Roofing, the mansion's portico roof no longer leaks after perhaps 30 years. The border of the portico roof is limestone, like the exterior walls of the house. But inside that border, a triangular piece of poured concrete, probably dating to the 1940s, was deteriorating due to roof leaks.

"Wagner removed the concrete and installed traffic surface waterproofing, and the leaks stopped," reports Briggs. As a bonus, the Briggses frequently use the newly repaired portico roof for relaxing and enjoying the streetscape below.

"Chuck Wagner has been great to work with. He has a good rapport with people," Briggs says. "And we've been very satisfied with the work Wagner Roofing has accomplished for us."

In the spring of 2014, Wagner Roofing replaced 6,627 square feet of rubber roofing on the main building and 400 linear feet of copper built-in gutter below the mansard.

🏛 **BELMONT MANSION (1909)**
**Architects: Ernest Sanson and Horace Trumbauer.
1618 New Hampshire Avenue NW. Skylights and
copper gutters were replaced.**

🏛 **BLAINE HOUSE (1881)**
Architect: John Fraser. 2000 Massachusetts Avenue NW.

Blaine Mansion

Blaine Mansion (1881) at Dupont Circle was constructed for House Speaker James G. Blaine and later owned by entrepreneur George Westinghouse.

Wagner Roofing's work in 1997 required a slate replacement of the mansard roof. It involved not only the removal of thousands of slates but the hand-cutting of their replacements, at the same 45-degree angle, to mirror the scalloped shape of the old slate. The mansion has three towers plus dormers, with multiple pitches, elevations, hips, and valleys.

"It was the challenge of all challenges in terms of a re-roofing job," Chuck Wagner says. "We took everything down to the bare wood and replaced it exactly as they had it."

A restored metal dormer.

CARSTARPHEN RESIDENCE (1881)
27 A Street SE. One of the company's more challenging jobs is what owner Dana Carstarphen calls "folk art," a house at Eighth and A streets SE, onto which Wagner Roofing installed new Vermont slate and copper finials, replicated three ornamental copper radiused dormer windows, and fabricated a copper built-in gutter.

Carstarphen, who bought the 1898 house with her husband in 2002, gave up her anniversary gifts "for the next 10 years" to have the copper made for the roof. The work "is a re-creation of exactly what was up there and lasted for 112 years," she says. "I think a lot of Capitol Hill restorations are cosmetic. To really get the right workmanship and historical accuracy, there's probably only one roofer in the whole city that can do it. And that's Wagner. I was never happier to write a check."

The Robert F. Kennedy Building

The U.S. Department of Justice Building (1934), now known as The Robert F. Kennedy Building, fills four square blocks between Pennsylvania and Constitution avenues and Ninth and 10th streets NW.

"We estimated the job would take 20 people" for the task, removing and refastening 72,000 square feet of sculpted clay roofing tiles and 51,000 square feet of flat roof "pavers" for the department's modernization project in 2005, Chuck Wagner says.

"This was not long after the terrorist attacks of 9/11. Security was unbelievably tight," Wagner says. "Basically they wouldn't let anyone close to that building unless they had the proper clearances."

The uniqueness of this job was the eave tile, known as antefixa, which is an ornamental tile that acts as a snow guard. The tiles on the ridge are known as finials. The replacement tile was made from samples from the roof. They are one of a kind and beautiful.

The Department of Justice would allow the 100-ton crane needed to hoist the heavy paver tiles up to the roof to come only on Saturdays, so as not to disrupt foot traffic.

The project took one year.

"We pulled it off," Sheila Wagner says. "The National Roofing Contractors Association recognized it as one of the jobs of the year with a Gold Circle Award. It gave us the confidence to do even bigger jobs, though at the time anything bigger was hard to imagine."

Antefixum detail.

🏛 **THE ROBERT F. KENNEDY BUILDING/U.S. DEPARTMENT OF JUSTICE (1934)**
Architect: Zantzinger, Borie & Medary. 950 Pennsylvania Avenue NW. General Contractor: Gilbane Building Company. Photo via wikipedia.com.

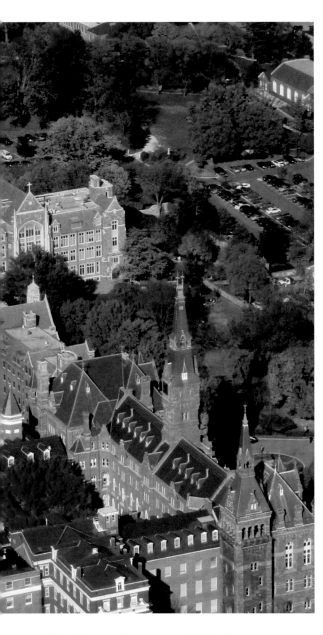

🏛 **GEORGETOWN UNIVERSITY'S
HEALY HALL (1877-1879)**
**3700 O Street NW. Designed by Paul Pelz and
John Smithmeyer in the neo-medieval style.**

Georgetown University's Healy Hall

Healy Hall (1879) is the flagship Georgetown University building with a signature clock tower that aircraft passengers on the left side of a plane can see as they twist their way down the Potomac River before landing at Reagan National Airport.

The job in 2008 included a replacement of the south side of Healy Hall's original slate roof, restoration of existing dormers, and installation of new gutters.

The project had its challenges. Even though the work was undertaken in summertime, the building was in use for classes. "They wanted us to be unobtrusive, out of sight" — if such a thing is possible up on a roof, Chuck Wagner says. "No trucks anywhere near the building, a net over our scaffold. We had a small sidewalk in the back we could walk through with our materials 100 yards to the site."

A second challenge involved access once Wagner's crew got to the rear of the building, which sat 10 feet below grade. Unable to bring materials to the base of the scaffold before "triple-handing" everything up, the company built a ramp from the street to the scaffold level.

Because of the brisk pedestrian traffic, "we went above and beyond in all of our safety precautions," Wagner says. The company installed safety netting on the sides and bottom of the scaffold; installed a full pedestrian tunnel around the rear entrance; fenced off access to the scaffold; and installed plywood at the bottom of the scaffold to prevent adventuresome students from gaining access at night.

"There comes a point — as it did with Wagner — when they were seeing what I was seeing in terms of quality and safety," commented Ron Bristol, construction superintendent for the contractor, Patner Construction. "At every point, our relationship was nothing short of fantastic."

Above, lead-coated copper ridge cap and a lightning rod are installed. At left, crew members tend to Healy Hall with Randy Herald, left, supervising the renovation.

OLD POST OFFICE BUILDING (1899)
Architect: Willoughby J. Edbrooke.
1100 Pennsylvania Avenue NW. Slate and
flashings were replaced on 17 dormers, copper
built-in gutter and water table; and masonry was
restored.

The Old Post Office

The Old Post Office Pavilion (1899), at 11th Street and Pennsylvania Avenue NW, is a romanesque 12-story colossus with a 315-foot, cathedral-like clock tower.

As Wagner Roofing restored masonry and replaced slate and flashings, safety was the highest priority. Copper was bent to fit the angle between two roof surfaces on 17 dormers.

"Maybe this work was our greatest accomplishment," Chuck Wagner says. "Concrete turrets had to be re-pointed. We did it without scaffolding by building a ring around the eight turrets. A special ladder was designed and hung from the rings, which rotated in a circle three times to do the masonry work."

Without scaffolding, Wagner employees moved around all four sides of the building, however, they took the elevator to the 12th floor and accessed the roof work area through the dormer windows.

In addition to the masonry, extensive metal work included replacing the built-in gutter with 20-ounce copper and the watertable below the gutter with 24-ounce lead-coated copper, which ran the perimeter of the building.

"It was extremely difficult work," noted Tony Cosentino, Wagner's superintendent on the job. "Getting the material to certain locations on the roof, and removing the debris, all without scaffolding, was the biggest challenge." A 100-ton crane made the deliveries. Safety railings were built, and everyone who worked on the steep roof and valleys wore safety lines not unlike a climber's belay system.

A General Services Administration architect called the company's copper installation "a work of art."

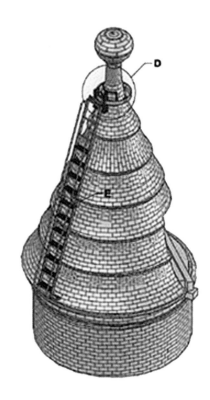

Above, finial restoration in process by Andrzej Tybor, who also fabricated the Star of David.

6th & I Historic Synagogue

The 6th & I Historic Synagogue (1907) was once the center of Jewish life in Washington. The first person married there was Arthur Welsh, a Wright brothers test pilot. After the migration of many congregants uptown, the Adas Israel congregation built a new sanctuary in the Cleveland Park neighborhood, and the historic synagogue was sold and reopened as an African Methodist Episcopal church in 1951. When that church, Turner Memorial, announced plans to move in 2002, Washington Wizards owner Abe Pollin and local developers Douglas Jemal and Shelton Zuckerman acquired the building for the Jewish community.

Wagner crews made periodic visits to the building for renovation projects large and small.

Wagner crews tell of unbelievable 120-degree heat reflecting off the new copper roofing below the four domes. The tile was removed from each dome, and rafters and supports called purlins were replaced at the Moorish-style house of worship by Wagner craftsmen in 2010. "Wagner's master craftsmen rebuilt the classic domes of this iconic building and coppered the roof to perfection," says John Stranix, whose firm represented the owner.

Chuck Wagner had helped his father with repairs there in 1959. "This building is a real Washington treasure," he says.

THE 6TH & I HISTORIC SYNAGOGUE (1907)
Architect: Louis Levi. 600 I Street NW. Tiles were removed, salvaged and relaid on the domes. Deteriorated rafters, purlins and sheathing under domes and metal roofs were replaced. New 20-ounce copper was installed on the flat portion of the roof, and 16-ounce standing-seam was installed over sloped portions. Abe Pollin, far left, Shelton Zuckerman, second from left, and Chuck Wagner, right, observe the Star of David being installed on the dome.

Shelton Zuckerman, second from right, congratulates Chuck Wagner and his team on the progress of the renovations. They are flanked by Bob Wooldridge and Lindsay Keiser.

🏛 **MARYLAND STATE HOUSE (1772)**
Architects: George A. Frederick and Joseph H. Anderson. 100 State Circle, Annapolis, Maryland. Atop the dome is a hand-carved wood version of the state fish: a rockfish.

MARYLAND STATE HOUSE
BUILT 1772-1779
CAPITOL OF THE UNITED STATES
NOVEMBER 26, 1783 - AUGUST 13, 1784
IN THIS STATE HOUSE, OLDEST IN THE NATION STILL
IN LEGISLATIVE USE, GENERAL GEORGE WASHINGTON
RESIGNED HIS COMMISSION BEFORE THE CONTINENTAL
CONGRESS DECEMBER 23, 1783. HERE, JANUARY 14, 1784,
CONGRESS RATIFIED THE TREATY OF PARIS TO END THE
REVOLUTIONARY WAR AND, MAY 7, 1784, APPOINTED
THOMAS JEFFERSON MINISTER PLENIPOTENTIARY. FROM
HERE, SEPTEMBER 14, 1786, THE ANNAPOLIS CONVENTION
ISSUED THE CALL TO THE STATES THAT LED TO THE
CONSTITUTIONAL CONVENTION.
A REGISTERED NATIONAL HISTORIC LANDMARK
MARYLAND HISTORICAL SOCIETY

The Maryland State House

The oldest state house (1772) — or state capitol — still in legislative use is actually two buildings, with one designed to match the architecture of the original structure added in 1902.

During a massive renovation in 1998, Wagner Roofing replaced all the slate on both buildings, restored the slate roof on the trademark dome, and installed new, lead-coated copper gutters. "For starters, we needed someone who could deal with anything they saw up there, including handling copper flashing" and other intricate roof anomalies, general contractor Tony Fiorini says.

"There are lots of people who could put down slate, but Wagner was brought on because we needed an outfit that could see the total picture," Fiorini says. "There are a lot of special needs in a project like this that people don't think about."

The job also posed an unusual challenge to Wagner crews and the 140 or so tradespeople from other contractors: The State House remained open for business. "Working in Annapolis on those little streets, crews of Wagner employees were out at 5 a.m. keeping traffic flowing," Chuck Wagner says. "State Circle, the main access to the building, was closed to allow a 100-ton crane to stock slate."

BELGIAN AMBASSADOR'S RESIDENCE (1931)
2300 Foxhall Road NW. Wagner Roofing performed work for Whiting-Turner Contracting Company, and the project architect was Quinn Evans Architects. New Buckingham slate, built-in copper gutters, and a batten-seam, terne-coated stainless-steel roof were installed. Wagner also replicated and installed radiused decorative molding on 15 copper dormers and window trim, which metal superintendent Bill Robin found especially interesting. "In order to fabricate them, we had to make special steel dies for each individual piece," he explains. Looking at the old metal, it was intriguing to see how earlier generations did their work. "We have a larger choice of tools," he says, "but we did most of the work just as they did, making our own dies, fabricating our own panels. The craftsmanship hasn't changed much."

President Lincoln's Cottage and the Robert H. Smith Visitor Education Center

President Lincoln's Cottage (1843), also known as Anderson Cottage, is at the Armed Forces Retirement Home in Northwest Washington.

Abraham Lincoln spent a quarter of his presidency in seclusion at this "summer White House," a forerunner of the Camp David retreat in the Maryland mountains. Built for George Washington Riggs, who would later found Riggs National Bank, and also used by Lincoln's predecessor, James Buchanan, the house fell into disrepair in the 20th century. It was purchased by the National Trust for Historic Preservation, which placed it on its "11 Most Endangered Places" list before undertaking a wholesale restoration, for which Wagner Roofing was engaged in 2005. The company installed a Vermont slate roof and a standing-seam, lead-coated copper roof on the cottage.

"We think this is one of the most important historical sites being restored in America today," says Richard L. Moe, president of the National Trust for Historic Preservation.

🏛 **NATIONAL TRUST FOR HISTORIC PRESERVATION'S ROBERT H. SMITH VISITOR EDUCATION CENTER AT THE SOLDIERS' HOME (1905)**
Architect: William Poindexter. Randolph Street and Rock Creek Church Road NW.
Designed and built to serve as the administration building for the Soldiers' Home.
Above, a statue of Abraham Lincoln watches over renovation work as shingle roof is removed and the same type of Spanish tile used in the original construction is being installed. At left, a photo by Jim Glaize of the completed work.

The Mormon Temple

The Mormon Temple (1968-74), also known as the Temple of the Church of Jesus Christ of Latter-day Saints, is a prominent landmark along a winding stretch of the Capital Beltway in Kensington, Maryland.

In 1995, Wagner Roofing employees carefully walked around scaffolding beside the temple's spired towers, rising 288 feet in the air. From their perch on a clear day, crews could see the distant mountains in Maryland and West Virginia. "We were eye level with passing birds and helicopters," one Wagner roofer reported.

"It was excellent scaffolding, the same used to clean the Statue of Liberty," Chuck Wagner says. "But we couldn't work on windy days. It was just too dangerous." Most of Wagner Roofing's work involved replacing copper flashing torn off by high winds.

The church's project manager wanted everything checked since "it will be a long time before scaffolding goes up again." In fact, all the roofing work was tested to be certain it was watertight before the scaffolding was removed.

CHURCH OF JESUS CHRIST OF LATTER-DAY SAINTS (MORMON TEMPLE) (1968-74)
Architect: Keith W. Wilcox. 9900 Stoneybrook Drive, Kensington, Maryland.

Tudor Place Foundation

SAVE AMERICA'S
TREASURES

The neoclassical Georgetown mansion Tudor Place (1816) was designed by William Thornton, the original architect of the U.S. Capitol, and built for Martha Custis Peter, a granddaughter of Martha Washington, and her husband, Thomas Peter. Today it is a National Historic Landmark.

The Carostead Foundation (later the Tudor Place Foundation) was started by the final owner, Armistead Peter III, and his wife, Caroline, in 1966.

Tudor Place is a treasure for its gardens and history. It has been called the best example of well-preserved neo-classical architecture in the nation, and visiting is free.

The Temple Portico is arguably the most prominent feature of the main house. Any caretaker of old buildings knows that moisture is an eternal enemy, and the painted tin roof had been letting some moisture seep in at the gutter line. Furthermore, the metal roof was on its last legs, heavily rusted and worn. Previous work on the roof in the past century had been limited to minor repairs and multiple layers of paint. The first tin roof lasted 68 years, and the second survived 128 years.

Wagner Roofing has inspected the mansion semiannually and maintained its roofing systems since the 1970s, thanks to a charitable trust established by Armistead Peter III. "We don't look at maintenance like an individual homeowner would," curator Chris Wilson said in 2002. "We are trying to preserve the house's historical significance, and the roofing elements are historical themselves. So we want to repair and replace them in kind."

Wilson said he was "impressed with the precision" of Wagner Roofing's work. "The estimator comes out and takes pictures with his digital camera, and when the workers arrive, they're carrying the photos with the trouble spots circled."

All metal roofs were replaced with lead-coated copper in 2008, and the temple portico dome structural repairs, built-in gutter, and lead-coated copper roof were completed in 2012.

Chuck Wagner says the new lead-coated copper roof, installed by Randy Herald, will last more than 200 years. "The biggest challenge on this job was the radiused work required on the built-in gutter and water table, which had to be installed in 18-inch sections," he says.

Every seam had to be soldered because new roof seams had to match the existing pattern down to an eighth of an inch.

🏛 **TUDOR PLACE (1816)**
Architect: William Thornton. 1644 31st Street NW. On opposite page, Temple Portico detail of radiused lead-coated built-in gutter, water table and flat-seam roof.

Washington National Cathedral

The Washington National Cathedral (construction was completed in 1990 — 83 years after it started) is the sixth-largest cathedral in the world and the fourth-tallest structure in Washington. Although it is an Episcopal house of worship, it was designated by Congress as "a national house of prayer" for people of all faiths.

The cathedral is 517 feet long and 301 feet at its highest point. One hundred fifty tons of masonry supports 1.5 acres of roofing which is drained by 112 gargoyles. Many of its 700,000 annual visitors come just to see its stained-glass windows, especially a west rose window made of 10,500 pieces of glass.

Wagner Roofing crews come and go up above, performing inspections and repairs as needed. "What's a cathedral without a scaffold?" says Joe Alonso, a stonemason who helped lay the great cathedral's last stone in 1990.

During one visit, in 2004, Wagner crews under Randy Herald removed six patches of a rubbery material that had been slapped on by someone to stanch leaks. "It looked terrible and was just a Band-Aid fix," Alonso said. "And so we replaced some batten-seam lead roofing."

For almost 20 years, Wagner crews have patrolled the roofs of all the facilities on the cathedral's "close," or campus, which includes St. Albans School and the Bishop's House. "Chuck employs great craftspeople," Alonso says, "from metalwork specialists like Randy to the workers who removed and replaced the Spanish-style tile roof on the carriage house for the National Cathedral [School] for girls, he's got the guys."

Alonso has had his hands full since an earthquake in August 2011, which damaged the cathedral. Without a major angel donation, scaffolding could remain on the building well after Alonso's retirement. Meanwhile, he is the perfect person to do this restoration since he knows every stone on the building.

🏛 **WASHINGTON NATIONAL CATHEDRAL (1907-1990)**
Architects: George Boydeley, Henry Vaughn and Philip Hurbert Frohman. 3101 Wisconsin Avenue NW. Above, Chuck Wagner and Joe Alonso, mason foreman.

HERB COTTAGE "OLD BAPTISTERY" (1904)
Architect: T Henry Randall. 3001 Wisconsin Avenue NW. Built before the construction of the National Cathedral as a temporary baptistery. By 1958, All Hallows Guild used it as an Herb Cottage. The slate roof, gutter, and flashings were replaced in 2005. After the 2011 earthquake, a 200-ton crane fell on the building; a section of the slate roof and the skylight were replaced with lead-coated copper.

Folger Building

This classic Beaux-Arts building, also known as the Hibbs Building, was built in 1908 and designed by Jules Henri de Sibour.

At the Folger Building — not the one housing a Shakespeare library but a gem that began its life on 15th Street NW as the home of Washington's first member of the New York Stock Exchange — Wagner crews replaced a failed structural roof deck, rebuilt copper cornices, replaced dormers, and installed new slate on the mansard roof in 2000 for Grunley Construction Company.

All windows were painted, and the exterior marble and damaged facade were repointed.

And Wagner Roofing had an unusual assignment: tearing out a "bird-removal system" from long ago and replacing it with modern StealthNet mesh that dissuades messy pigeons from landing. Previous "bird anchor" systems involved drilling holes into the building facade and inserting ferrous bolts, which rusted, expanded, and fractured the building's stone — 100 feet above pedestrians passing below.

Other work at Folger included the design and remodeling of interior offices on two floors. Rachel Wagner, the youngest daughter of Chuck and Sheila Wagner, produced the design for the project as an associate architect.

U.S. DEPARTMENT OF TREASURY (1836)
Architect: Robert Mills. 1500 Pennsylvania Avenue NW. Neoclassical style. Wagner replaced lead-coated copper flashing in 2000. General Contractor: Grunley Construction Company.

🏛 **FOLGER BUILDING (1908)**
Architect: Jules Henri de Sibour. 725 15th
Street NW. Above photo of completed work via
wikipedia.com. At left, masons and painters in the
center of the photo and Chuck Wagner inspects
the cornice at the top right.

43

Kreeger Museum

The roof replacement on the Kreeger Museum (1967) on Foxhall Road was daunting on several fronts. The museum, designed by Philip Johnson and Richard Foster, houses 200 works from the Carmen and David Lloyd Kreeger art collection in an unusual building.

It features 15 modern domes over cube-shaped rooms that measure 22 feet per side. Flowing arches with walls of cut travertine are accented by teak and anodized aluminum. And, as Wagner project manager Lee Simon notes, a major consideration was the sheer value of what lay inside. "A single drop of water entering the building during the replacement was unacceptable," he says.

The original roof structure consisted of six inches of poured concrete and two inches of lightweight concrete. Wagner Roofing removed the lightweight layer to install insulation and a new rubber membrane on the domes.

"We found a one-inch insulation that will bend and contour to the dome," said Marc Graver, the museum's operations manager. "When you work with domes, you can't just lay something flat on top." The domes were then covered with new 90-mil 30-year Firestone rubber roofing.

Wagner Roofing's work was featured in the July 2006 issue of Professional Roofing magazine. "It was of the utmost importance for the museum to engage a roofing company that could deal with the complexities of the architectural design," Judy Greenberg, the museum's director, says of the complicated project, which was completed even as Kreeger continued to welcome tours and educational programs.

KREEGER MUSEUM (1967)
Architects: Philip Johnson and Richard Foster. 2401 Foxhall Road NW.

Fransican Monastery

The Franciscan Monastery in Northeast Washington was designed in 1899 by Aristide Leonori in the Byzantine revival and gothic style. In 2009, the challenge was more than a roof replacement. It required mathematical as well as roofing skills.

The monastery's beautiful copper dome had been leaking so badly that, at one point, 38 buckets were catching the rain below. It wasn't the first rush project that Wagner Roofing field superintendent Dan Williams had encountered, but it was the trickiest, because the dome is more egg-shaped than round. "One hundred years ago, it was tough to make a perfect circle," Williams says. "I had to dust off some old-school notebooks and remind myself how to do trigonometry" in order to cover the oddly shaped dome with equal-size copper pans.

🏛 **FRANSICAN MONASTERY (1899)**
Architect: Aristide Leonori. 1400 Quincy Street NE.

Gallagher Mansion

Built between 1854 and 1857, the Italianate villa is named after Patrick Gallagher, a grocer with a large family who hired architect Edmund Lind to expand the house to 17 rooms in around 1879. Gallagher added a third story with a mansard roof that reflects the French Second Empire style. The home stayed in the Gallagher family for 99 years, until 1972, but deteriorated rapidly after that because of neglect and vandalism.

The City of Baltimore bought the dilapidated building in 1986 in the hopes of saving this landmark, which is on the National Register of Historic Places. With $3.4 million secured in 1995, restoration work began.

Restoring the ornate slate mansard roof became the challenge for Wagner Roofing. As slate veteran Bob Wooldridge says, "As far as degree of difficulty from one to 10, it was right up there in the eight category."

This job represents a complete transformation of a pre-Civil War-era home. Working for General Contractor Harkins Builders, Inc., Wagner Roofing's part involved removing the original pattern of the slate roof so that it could be relaid exactly as it was. Once this was accomplished, multicolored, scallop-shaped slate that encircles the steep mansard roof was laid using salvaged red and green Vermont slate and Buckingham slate. In addition, a new stainless-steel roof was installed, as well as gutters and downspout.

For Wooldridge's work on this project, he received the Craftsmanship Award from the Building Congress and Exchange of Metropolitan Baltimore. Project architect Harry Hess says, "Wagner's job is one of the best I've ever seen."

Before

During

Embassies & Official Residences

EMBASSY OF CAMEROON (1906), ON OPPOSITE PAGE
2349 Massachusetts Avenue NW. George Totten Jr. designed the building in the beaux-arts style for Norwegian diplomat Christian Hauge. Wagner replaced the copper built-in gutter, mansard roofs, and standing-seam copper on the main roof as well as installing lead-coated copper finials and completing major structural repairs.

RESIDENCE OF THE AMBASSADOR OF THE NETHERLANDS (1929), AT LEFT
2347 S Street NW. The neoclassical revival design is both the ambassador's residence and a private museum. Everything above the gutter line was replaced, including the slate mansard and flat roof above the mansard with stainless steel.

EMBASSY OF SWAZILAND (1892)
1712 New Hampshire Avenue NW. Architect Thomas Franklin Schneider designed the building in the Richardsonian romanesque style with Moorish detailing. Schneider's most famous work was the Cairo Apartment Building on Q Street NW. The tile roof on the turret and mansard was relaid, and the flat roof was replaced with 20-year rubber roofing.

🏛 **TAIPEI'S ECONOMIC & CULTURAL OFFICE (REPUBLIC OF CHINA) TWIN OAKS (1888)**
3225 Woodley Road NW. The building was designed in the colonial Georgian revival style by Francis Allen for Gardiner Green Hubbard, founder and first president of the National Geographic Society and father-in-law of Alexander Graham Bell. It is the only remaining example of this style in the District. It is known as Twin Oaks for the largest such trees in Washington. Wagner rebuilt and repointed four chimneys, restored the slate roof, replaced the copper roof, gutters and snowguards, as well as, completing interior structural work, drywall, and painting.

🏛 **BRITISH EMBASSY (1928)**
3100 Massachusetts Avenue NW. Architect Sir Edwin Lutyens mixed Queen Anne with art moderne. New copper and 20-year membrane roofs were installed, and the tile roof restored.

Museums

🏛 **CORCORAN GALLERY OF ART (1869)**
Architect: Ernest Flagg. 500 17th Street NW. Wagner performed triage roof repairs for the Christman Company. All roof leaks were stopped for the first time in 20 years.

U.S. BOTANIC GARDEN CONSERVATORY (1933), ABOVE
Architect of the Capitol. 100 Maryland Avenue SW. A weir, which raises water flow and diverts water from gutters to hydrate the plants, was installed. The garden established in 1820 is oldest botanic garden in North America.

SMITHSONIAN CASTLE(1846 TO 1855), AT LEFT
1000 Jefferson Drive SW. The castle was designed by James Renwick Jr. in the gothic style with romanesque motifs. The cornerstone was laid by President Polk in 1855. Wagner performed slate repairs, valley, and metal roof replacement on the main building, and replaced the lead-coated copper skylight over the Commons Room. When lightning struck the southeast tower, at left, Wagner performed structural repairs and restored the slate roof. In the background, the Arts and Industries Building.

NATIONAL AIR AND SPACE MUSEUM (1976), ABOVE
Architect: Gyo Obata. 600 Independence Avenue SW. With more than 9 million visitors annually, this Smithsonian Institution museum holds the largest collection of historic aircraft and spacecraft in the world. The terraced roof above the "Apollo to the Moon" exhibit was replaced with a green roof.

RENWICK GALLERY/SMITHSONIAN (1859 TO 1863), AT RIGHT
1661 Pennsylvania Avenue NW .The gallery was designed by James Renwick Jr. in the Second Empire style . The copper built-in gutter and drains were replaced.

LIBRARY OF CONGRESS, MADISON BUILDING KIOSK (1990)

101 Independence Avenue SE. The kiosk, cupola, and finials were fabricated in the Wagner shop. The copper roof, batten caps, cupola, and finial were installed on site. The kiosk was designed to replicate the cupola on the roof of the Library of Congress.

SAVE AMERICA'S TREASURES

🏛 **WOODLAWN PLANTATION (1800-1805)**
9000 Richmond Highway, Alexandria, Virginia. Originally part of Mount Vernon, it was designed by William Thornton, Architect of the Capitol, at the request of President Washington for his step-granddaughter, Martha Parke-Custis. Wagner installed new Buckingham slate and copper roofs, replaced gutters and downspouts, repointed five brick chimneys, replaced wood railings and painted all trim, as well as restoring the historic bell. The lightning rod system was replaced. Architect: Davis Buckley Architects & Planners. Project Manager: Tom Striegel.

🏛 **CARLYLE HOUSE (1753)**
121 North Fairfax Street, Alexandria, Virginia. Scottish merchant John Carlyle had the house built in the Georgian Palladian style. Fire retardant scallop-cut cedar shingles with two coats of paint were installed for the current owner, Northern Virginia Regional Park Authority.

🏛 ARTS AND INDUSTRIES BUILDING (1879),
ABOVE AND LEFT
**900 Jefferson Drive SW. Adolf Cluss designed the
building in the late Victorian style. The metal roof
was restored.**

🏛 PHILLIPS HOUSE, PART OF THE PHILLIPS COLLECTION (1897)
1600 21st Street NW. Duncan Phillips, who built the house for his family, played a seminal role in introducing America to modern art. The copper built-in gutter and slate mansard roof were replaced.

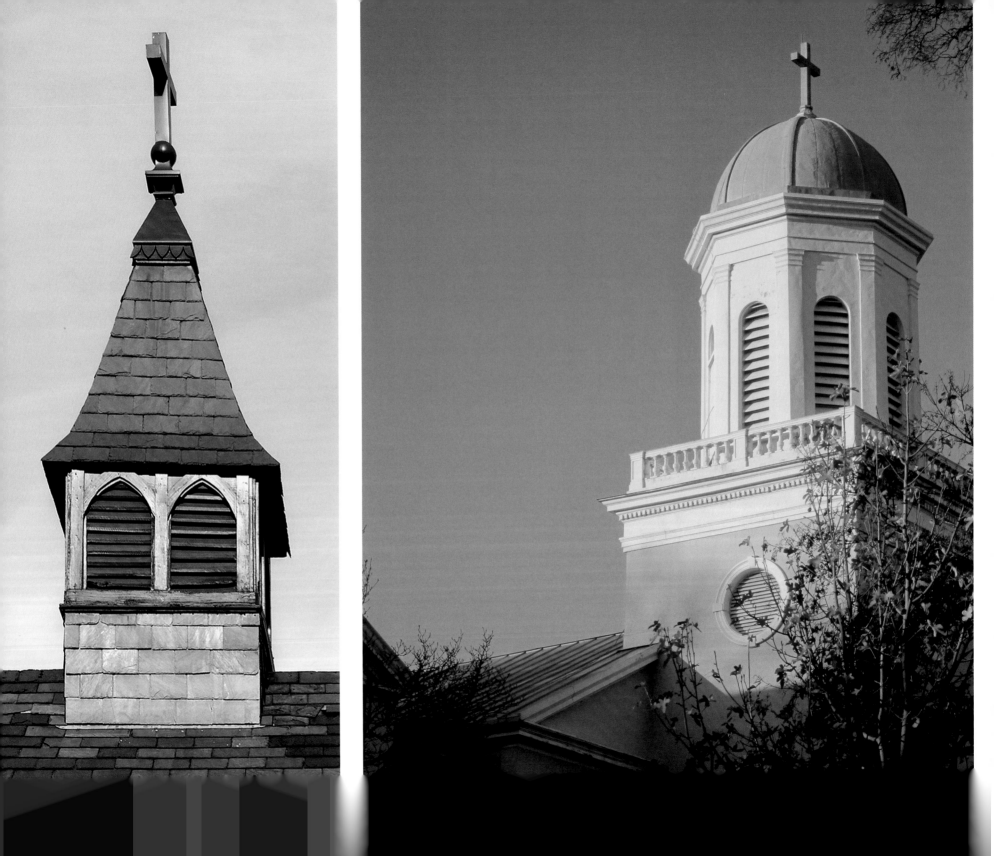

Houses of Worship

🏛 **SAINT MARY'S EPISCOPAL CHURCH (1887), AT FAR LEFT**
728 23rd Street NW. James Renwick Jr. designed the church in the gothic revival style. This was the first African American Episcopal congregation in Washington. The slate roof was restored, and structural repairs to the cupola were made.

SAINT JOHN'S EPISCOPAL CHURCH GEORGETOWN (1804), MIDDLE
3240 O Street NW. The copper built-in gutter was replaced, structural repairs were made, and new slate and 90-mil, 30-year rubber roofs were installed.

🏛 **LUTHER PLACE MEMORIAL CHURCH (1870), AT LEFT**
1226 Vermont Avenue NW. The church was designed by architects Judson York, J.C. Harkness, and Henry Davis in the neogothic style. The slate roof and finials on the towers were replaced, the built-in gutter was restored, and the flat roof on the annex was replaced. Structural damage and slate on the steeple were repaired.

🏛 **CHURCH OF THE ASCENSION AND SAINT AGNES (1874)**

1215 Massachusetts Avenue NW. Architects Charles Carson and Thomas Dixon of Baltimore designed the church in the Victorian gothic style. It reached a height of 74 feet with a 190-foot tower and spire that was visible across much of the city. The interior features cast-iron columns and timber trusses and was illuminated by gas lamps. Wagner replaced the built-in gutters on the main church and restored the spire that was damaged by an earthquake in 2011. This work consisted of replacing wood and steel beams, precast carved stone, and copper roofing. The same approach to the structural repairs was used at the National Cathedral.

NATIONAL PRESBYTERIAN CHURCH (1967)
4101 Nebraska Avenue NW. Harold Wagoner designed the church in the modernist neogothic style. Wagner replaced lead-coated copper built-in gutter and copper roofs.

🏛 **NATIONAL CITY CHRISTIAN CHURCH** (1930)
5 Thomas Circle NW. The church was designed by John Russell Pope (who also designed the Jefferson Memorial and National Archives) in the neoclassical style. Wagner restored the gutter and installed the flat roof.

🏛 **SAINT JOHN'S EPISCOPAL CHURCH ON LAFAYETTE SQUARE** (1815)
1525 H Street NW. Known as the "Church of the Presidents," it was designed by Benjamin Latrobe. The copper gutters and downspouts on the church were replaced, the church roof was repaired. The structure on the overhang and the copper built-in gutter on the parish house were replaced.

FOUNDRY UNITED METHODIST CHURCH (1903)
Architect: Appleton P. Clark. 1500 16th Street NW. New lead-coated copper built-in gutters and cornice were replaced, and 13,000 square feet of new Buckingham slate was installed.

DAHLGREN CHAPEL OF THE SACRED HEART AT GEORGETOWN UNIVERSITY (DEDICATED IN 1893)
37th and O Streets NW. The slate roof was relaid, and the copper gutters and downspouts were replaced.

🏛 **CONGRESSIONAL CEMETERY CHAPEL(1903), ABOVE**
Architect: Benjamin Latrobe.1801 E Street SE.
For 70 years the cemetery served as the country's national cemetery. 19 senators and 71 congressional representatives are buried here, as well as 10 mayors of Washington and John Philip Sousa. The existing slate roof was relaid, and the built-in gutter was replaced. The windows and ridge cornice were restored.

HOLY APOSTLES ORTHODOX CHURCH (1880), AT LEFT
6011 Ammendale Road, Beltsville, Maryland. The church was formerly Saint Joseph's Church, built by Adm. Daniel Ammen (a naval officer in the Civil War) in the American Queen Anne Revival style. He was childhood friend of President Grant who rescued a young Grant from drowning. The standing-seam tin roof was restored. A new lead-coated copper cross was fabricated and installed to match the existing cross.

METROPOLITAN MEMORIAL UNITED METHODIST CHURCH (1932), AT RIGHT

3401 Nebraska Avenue NW. Installed a new spire and cross above the base of the steeple.

GRACE REFORMED CHURCH (1892-1903), OPPOSITE PAGE

1405 15th Street NW. Paul J. Pelz designed the church in the late gothic revival style. Theodore Roosevelt was a member during his presidency, and he laid the cornerstone. Wagner performed maintenance and miscellaneous repairs to slate, gutters, and masonry from 2000 to 2012.

DOWNTOWN BAPTIST CHURCH (1954), AT RIGHT
212 South Washington Street, Alexandria, Virginia. Wagner installed new hand-cut, diamond-shaped Buckingham and Vermont slate on the eight-sided, 100-foot-high steeple to match the original design.

BASILICA OF THE NATIONAL SHRINE OF THE IMMACULATE CONCEPTION (1920-1961), ON OPPOSITE PAGE
Architect: Charles Donagh Maginnis. 400 Michigan Avenue NE. The shrine is the largest Catholic church in the United States, the largest church of any kind in the western hemisphere, the eighth-largest church building in the world, and the tallest habitable building in Washington, D.C. It is a blend of Romanesque and Byzantine styles. Wagner relaid the tile roofs on six bay windows.

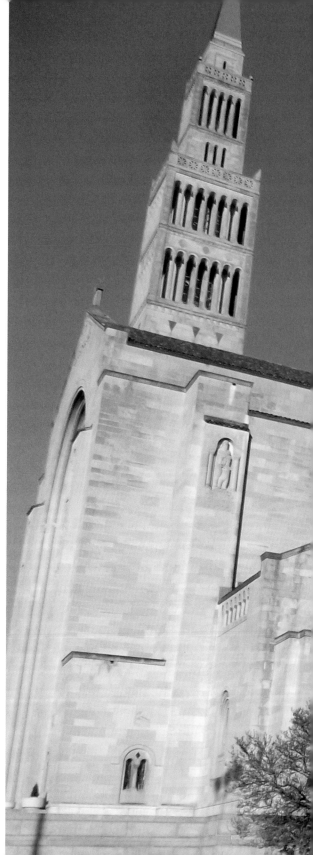

DOMINICAN HOUSE OF STUDIES (1905)
Architects for the addition: DeLizzio Seligson
Architects & Planners. 487 Michigan Avenue NE.
The building is in the Gothic style. A new
synthetic slate roof on the addition was installed
for Whiting-Turner Contracting Company.

Ship's wheel being fabricated.

Crew putting finishing touches on the cupola.

Original and replicated copper finials.

Original cupola used as template to fabricate the new roof.

CAPITOL HILL SEVENTH-DAY ADVENTIST CHURCH (1909)
914 Massachusetts Avenue NE. The cornerstone was set by President Taft. Wagner replaced 4500 square feet of copper; and replicated the copper cupola, finials, and the ship's wheel on top.

Schools & Universities

UNIVERSITY OF VIRGINIA ROTUNDA (1826)
Architect: Thomas Jefferson. 1826 University Avenue, Charlottesville, Virginia. Photo by Skyshots Photography.

UNIVERSITY OF VIRGINIA ROTUNDA (1826)
Construction began in 1822 and was completed in 1826 at a cost of almost $60,000. Designed by Thomas Jefferson, who did not live to see its completion, it was the last building on the Lawn to be completed. Working under Gilbane/Christman Company and WA Lynch Company, Wagner fabricated and installed copper roofing.

CATHOLIC UNIVERSITY OF AMERICA'S CALDWELL HALL (1888), ABOVE AND AT LEFT
Architect: E. Francis Baldwin. 620 Michigan Avenue NE. Restored the wind-damaged copper finial in the shop and reinstalled it using a 50-ton crane and a 100-foot manlift.

🏛 **FRANKLIN SCHOOL (1869), ON OPPOSITE PAGE**
Project Architect: Mary Oehrlein. 925 13th Street NW. General Contractor: Sigal Construction. Designed by Adolf Cluss, a German-born American immigrant who became one of the most important architects in Washington, D.C., in the late 19th century. Wagner installed handcut Vermont slate, radiused lead-coated chimney caps, 24-ounce lead-coated copper gutters, gold-leaf finials and a weathervane.

LAB SCHOOL/CLARK HOUSE (1893)

4759 Reservoir Road NW. General Contractor: Sigal Construction. Built in the gothic revival style using red sandstone. The Clarks lived in the house until 1923, when it became the Florence Crittenton Home for Unwed Mothers. The Lab School purchased the building in 1976. Wagner replaced the slate roof and built-in gutters, as well as replicated the finials. The old finials are shown at right.

MARET SCHOOL, WOODLEY MANSION (1801), ABOVE
3000 Cathedral Avenue NW. Built by Phillip Barton Key in the Federal style and once home to Grover Cleveland, Martin Van Buren and Gen. George Patton. Wagner has maintained the mansion roof and all buildings on campus for over 30 years.

MARET SCHOOL, STURTEVANT ACADEMIC CENTER, AT LEFT
Wagner replaced the skylight shown.

🏛 **GALLAUDET UNIVERSITY PRESIDENT'S HOME** (1869)
Architect: Frederick Withers. Wagner restored the slate roof and gutters on the 35-room Victorian gothic mansion.

🏛 **GALLAUDET UNIVERSITY, OLE JIM (1881)**
Architect: Frederick Withers. Wagner restored the slate roof and gutters.

🏛 GALLAUDET UNIVERSITY, CHAPEL HALL (1870), ABOVE AND AT LEFT

Architect: Frederick Withers. 800 Florida Avenue NE. Chapel Hall, in the Ruskinian gothic revival style, is one of the finest examples of post-Civil War collegiate architecture. Wagner recorded the existing slate layout including exposures, design, and coursing to preserve the color patterns to replicate the original design with new Buckingham and Vermont slate. Project Architect: Einhorne Yaffee Prescott Architecture & Engineering.

WASHINGTON INTERNATIONAL SCHOOL (1914)
3100 Macomb Street NW. Charles Platt designed the estate, also known as Tregaron, in the beaux-art country style shown in rendering at right. Wagner replaced the structural overhang on all sides of the mansion and replaced copper gutter.

TRUTH, CRANDALL, FRAZIER, AND WHEATLEY HALLS (1931) AT HOWARD UNIVERSITY
2400 Sixth Street NW. Albert Irvin Cassell was a prominent mid-20th-century African-American architect in Washington, D.C., and he spent 20 years at Howard University. The Vermont slate roofs and copper cupolas were replaced on all buildings.

🏛 **NATIONAL CATHEDRAL SCHOOL, HEARST HALL (1900)**
3612 Woodley Road NW. Robert W. Gibson designed the school in the French chateau style, and Adolf Cluss supervised the construction. Wagner replaced four circular copper dormer windows and the remaining A-frame and radiused decorative copper on the dormers at the west elevation. Replaced the copper built-in gutter and valleys, and restored the Vermont slate roof on the east, west and south elevations.

A statue of George Washington, above, in the University Quadrangle.

🏛 GEORGE WASHINGTON UNIVERSITY, STOCKTON HALL (1925), AT RIGHT
Architects; Albert Harris and Arthur Heaton. 716 20th Street NW. The hall was the second building erected on the campus. Wagner replaced the tin roof with standing-seam copper. Ventilators and lead-coated copper railings were replicated, and the cupola was restored and painted.

GEORGE WASHINGTON UNIVERSITY, ABOVE
2100 Foxhall Road NW. West Hall at the Mount Vernon campus was built by Donohoe Construction as a residence hall. LEED-certified synthetic slate and TPO membrane roofs were installed.

Clubs

🏛 **WASHINGTON CLUB: PATTERSON MANSION (1903)**

15 Dupont Circle NW. Stanford White designed the house in the Neoclassical style for Robert Wilson Patterson, who was the editor of the Chicago Tribune. Charles Lindbergh stayed in the house in 1927 after his triumphant transatlantic flight. The copper roof and valleys were replaced, and a 20-year membrane roof was installed on the annex.

CONGRESSIONAL COUNTRY CLUB (1924)
Architect: Philip M. Jullien. General contractor: Coakley & Williams Construction. 8500 River Road, Bethesda, Maryland. Wagner installed Spanish tile, copper gutter and downspouts on the fitness center addition, pool pavilion cabana, stone bar and terrace addition, as well as a modified bitumen roof on the fitness center. Wagner has

COLUMBIA COUNTRY CLUB (1911)
7900 Connecticut Avenue, Chevy Chase, Maryland. The original clubhouse was designed by Frederick Pyle. The Spanish tile on the main clubhouse roof was relaid, and the flat roof was replaced in 1980. Photos at left clockwise, tile was installed on the men's locker room, fitness center and tennis house in 2011. Work was performed for Coakley & Williams Construction. The flat roofs on the ballroom, dining room and Gold Room were replaced with LEED-certified TPO.

🏛 ARTS CLUB (1806)
2015 and 2017 I Street NW. Built in the Federal style, it is where President Monroe lived after the British burned the White House in 1812. Wagner replaced the slate and tin roof and installed copper gutters and downspouts.

🏛 COSMOS CLUB (1898-1900), ABOVE AND AT LEFT

Architect: Carrere and Hastings. 2121 Massachusetts Avenue NW. In 1950, the Cosmos Club, a private social and cultural organization whose members are eminent in their professional fields, purchased the beaux-art-style property. The copper cornice on the mansard roof, the copper roof, and skylights on the main roof and library were replaced, as well as the tin roof on the Warne Lounge. New membrane roofs were installed over the dining room and Powell Auditorium.

CAR BARN (1897)

3520 Prospect Street NW. Waddy Wood designed the Georgetown site, originally known as Union Station, for the Capital Traction Company. He also designed the Woodrow Wilson House. The pavers were removed and relaid over 8000 square feet of 20-year membrane roofing for Douglas Jemal.

Historic

WHITE HOUSE (1792 AND 1800)

Architect: James Hoban. 1600 Pennsylvania Avenue NW. Hoban was chosen in a design competition that received nine proposals, including one submitted anonymously by Thomas Jefferson. At right, Wagner crew members perform repairs over the Oval Office press briefing room during the Nixon administration. President Nixon had more than roof leaks.

U.S. CAPITOL (1793)
Architect: William Thornton. First Street SE. Cast-iron repairs were made during Phase 1 of the Skirt Project for Gilbane/Christman Company.

DAUGHTERS OF THE AMERICAN REVOLUTION CONSTITUTION HALL (1929), AT RIGHT AND FAR RIGHT

311 18th Street NW. John Russell Pope designed the building in the monumental neoclassical style. 380 feet of copper cornice and 68 stamped copper crests were replaced. Work was performed under the direction of Roof Consulting Services.

MEMORIAL CONTINENTAL HALL (1904-10), ABOVE AND AT RIGHT

Architect: Edward Pearce Casey. 1776 D Street NW. The building is operated by the Daughters of the American Revolution. The lead-coated copper built-in gutter on the water table was replaced under the direction of the Christman Companies, the general contractor.

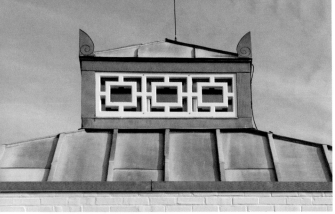

WALDRON FAULKNER HOUSE (1937)

3415 36th Street NW. The house was designed by Waldron Faulkner in the art moderne style. He designed the hardware, light fixtures, and furniture. Wagner replaced the batten-seam copper roof and the built-in gutter with pre-patinaed copper. At left, four copper antefixa on the cupola were replicated and installed.

SUMMER HOUSE (1879-81)

Located in the west front of the U.S. Capitol and built in the form of a hexagon. Designed by Frederick Law Olmstead, it was used as a cooling-off area by members of Congress before the Capitol had air conditioning. Stone benches provide seating for 22 people, and a fountain provided drinking water piped from a spring. The red brickwork is laid in geometric and artistic patterns and takes on a basket-weave appearance. All brick and tile were handmade. Wagner relaid the roof and installed copper flashings.

🏛 **ANDREW MELLON BUILDING, NATIONAL TRUST FOR HISTORIC PRESERVATION (1915)**
1785 Massachusetts Avenue NW. Jules Henri de Sibour designed the building in the beaux-arts style. Built by Stanley McCormick, it was one of Washington's first luxury apartment buildings. Wagner has maintained the roof from 1976 when the National Trust moved in, working on the built-up roof, slate mansard and built-in gutters.

HALCYON HOUSE (1787)
3400 Prospect Street NW. The house was built and designed by the first secretary of the Navy, Benjamin Stoddert. New Buckingham slate and copper roofing was installed. The restoration won a D.C. Preservation League Award.

🏛 **SOCIETY OF THE CINCINNATI, ANDERSON HOUSE (1905)**
Architects: Little and Browne. 2118 Massachusetts Avenue NW. The copper built-in gutter was replaced and the slate roof restored.

🏛 **OAK HILL CEMETERY RENWICK CHAPEL (1850)**
Architect: James Renwick Jr. 3001 R Street NW. The Chapel is the only known example of Renwick's Gothic Revival ecclesiastical design in Washington, DC. Wagner replaced the purple Vermont slate roof and replaced the copper built-in gutter and downspouts. Inset photo of job in progress by Dave Jackson, Oak Hill Cemetery superintendent.

DELANEY BUILDING (CIRCA 1789)
131 North Washington Street, Alexandria, Virginia. Christ Church steeple is in the background. Wagner replaced the slate roof on the mansard, installed new copper on the main roof, and painted all trim.

BAUMAN FOUNDATION, JEWETT HOUSE (1905)
Architect: Marsh & Peter. 2040 S Street NW. Built in the English Georgian style, the mansion's Ludiwici French roof tile was relaid. The copper built-in gutters and radius standing-seam copper dormers were replaced. Four chimneys were repointed, new dormer windows were fabricated and installed, and all exterior wood surfaces were painted.

🏛 **ROBERT E. LEE BOYHOOD HOME (1795)**
607 Oronoco Street, Alexandria, Virginia. The house was built in the Federal architectural style. Robert Lee lived here until he went to West Point. The slate roof was replaced.

🏛 **MAXWELL WOODHULL HOUSE, GEORGE WASHINGTON UNIVERSITY (1855)**
2033 G Street NW. The house was built in the Italianate style for Maxwell Woodhull, who was a commander in the U.S. Navy. He donated the house to George Washington University in 1921. Major structural repairs were made, a new standing-seam copper roof was installed, and all the windows were restored and painted.

AMERICAN RED CROSS (1915-17)
Architects: Trowbridge & Livingston. 430 17th Street
NW. The green glazed roof tile and copper built-in
gutters were replaced.

JACKSON (SCHOOL) ART CENTER IN GEORGETOWN (1890)

3048 R Street NW. Jackson School is one of nine historic schools in Georgetown. It is now used as an art center. Wagner's work included slate repair, hip and valley replacement, built-in gutter repair, metal cornice restoration, and painting. The flat roof was replaced with 20-year rubber.

🏛 BOWIE SEVIER HOUSE (1808)

3124 Q Street NW. It is a Federal-style mansion in the Historic Georgetown District built by Washington Bowie, the godson of George Washington. Renovation took 2.5 years. The Peach Bottom slate roof, which has a 200 -year life span, was relaid. Wagner installed lead-coated copper roofs on the two main house wings, the guest house, and the new pool house. General contractor: Gibson Builders. Project manager: Buddy Zeigler.

🏛️ **U.S. NAVAL ACADEMY ADMINISTRATION BUILDING (1898)**
Architect: Ernest Flagg. 121 Blake Road, Annapolis, Maryland. Wagner, working under Whiting-Turner Contracting Company, replaced slate and copper roofs and the skylight on the beaux-art-style building. Slate and standing-seam copper were installed on the addition. On opposite page, the front of the Administration Building, showing new copper built-in gutter and downspouts. Project Architect: Randy Ghertler.

STAUNTON HILL FARM (1848)
1100 Magnolia Lane, Brookneal, Virginia. A
castellated gothic mansion. Wagner replaced 6,800
square feet of copper roofing.

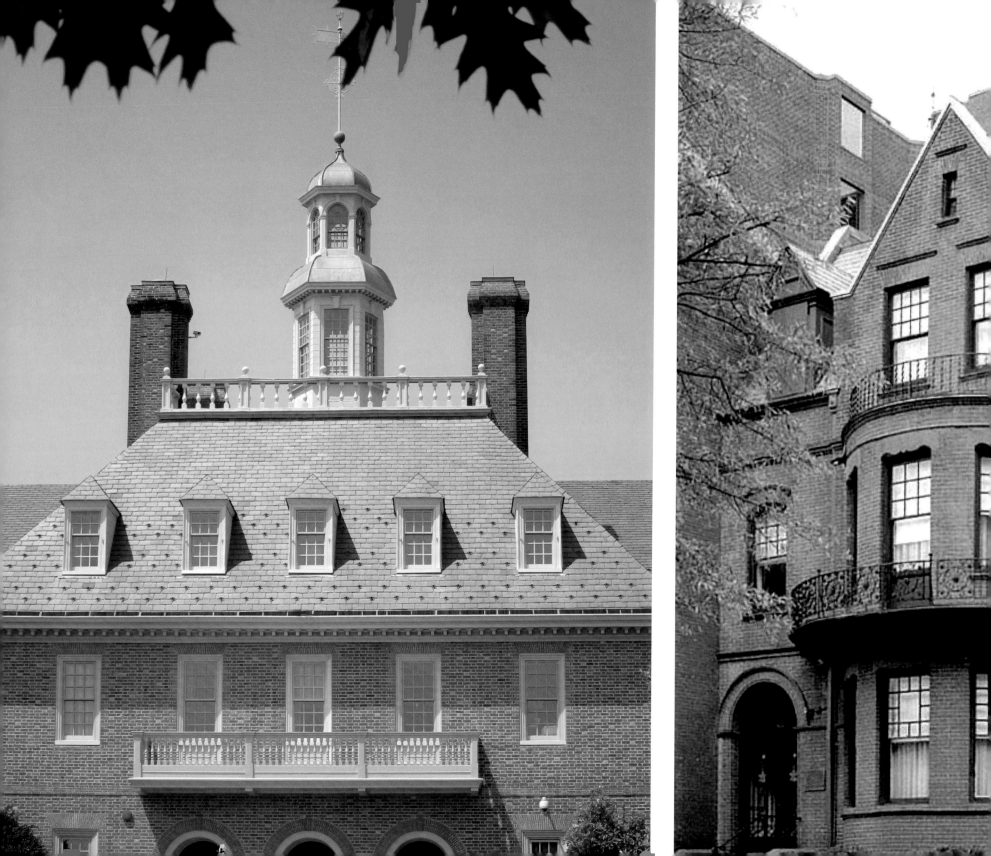

Commercial

FANNIE MAE (1956), OPPOSITE PAGE
3900 Wisconsin Avenue, NW. It was designed by Leon Chatelain Jr. in the Colonial revival style. Under the direction of Roof Consulting Services, Wagner replaced 2,800 linear feet of copper built-in gutter on the 1956, 1963, and 1977 buildings. All windows were painted and caulked, and all drains were replaced.

🏛 **NATIONAL SOCIETY, U.S. DAUGHTERS OF 1812 (1884), AT LEFT**
1463 Rhode Island Avenue NW. Also called the Admiral John Henry Upshur House, it was designed by Frederick Withers in the Queen Anne style. It was purchased for $31,000 in 1918. The slate and copper roofs were replaced, major structural repairs were made, and the chimney was restored.

COLUMBIA HOSPITAL FOR WOMEN (1916)/COLUMBIA RESIDENCES (2008)
2425 L Street NW. Designed by Nathan C. Wyeth in the Italianate style. The design highlights the importance of light and air in medical thinking of the day. For a century and a half, the Columbia Hospital for Women was the city's birthplace of choice for all races and was chartered by Congress in 1866. The hospital was the birthplace of about 275,000 individuals, including Jack and Chuck Wagner. The glazed tile roof was restored, and the copper and modified bitumen roofs were replaced.

AMERICAN COLLEGE OF OBSTETRICIANS AND GYNECOLOGISTS (1989), AT LEFT AND ABOVE
Architect: Arthur Cotton Moore. 409 12th Street SW. Installed new standing-seam copper over the original concrete deck under the supervision of Daniel Karchem, building consultant.

PIZZERIA PARADISO
3282 M Street NW. A LEED-certified 20-year TPO roof was installed for Synder Properties.

🏛 **APPLE STORE**
1229 Wisconsin Avenue NW. A flat-seam, stainless-steel roof and LEED-certified 20-year TPO roof were installed.

🏛 **GEORGETOWN**
30th and M Streets NW. A new Buckingham slate roof was installed.

CLYDE'S

Above, Samuel French Tavern (1804), 42920 Broadlands Boulevard, Ashburn, Virginia.

Upper right, Chandler Barn (1885), Synthetic slate and modified bitumen and lead-coated copper roofs were installed on four buildings dating from 1780 to 1885. These structures were moved to the Virginia site from Vermont.

At right, Clyde's office headquarters in Georgetown, 3236 M Street, NW. The tin roof was replaced with pre-painted steel, and major structural repairs were made.

TOWER OAKS LODGE

In appreciation for the opportunity to construct the Tower Oaks Lodge, Maizel Construction wishes to recognize
the Clyde's Restaurant Group, known for unsurpassed service, fine fare and incomparable ambiance.
Congratulations on your latest addition to the area's finest restaurants.

&

Special thanks to: the CRG design team, John Laytham, President;
Tom Meyer, Executive V.P.; Jeff Owens, CFO; Gregg Schipa, Chief Designer; Chatelain Architects; Persona Inc.; Bob Mortensen; and
Maizel Construction, Inc., General Contractor, Gordon MacDonald, Superintendent.

&

We would also like to recognize the following whose perseverance and craftsmanship made this building truly extraordinary:

ontracting	Standard Supply
Enterprises	Stewart Caulking
Studio	Strickland Fire Protection
Kinney	Superior Carpet
by Design	The City of Rockville
)S	Tissot Construction
nstruction	W and W Electric
Painting	Wagner Roofing

TOWER OAKS LODGE
**2 Preserve Parkway, Rockville, Maryland.13,100
square feet of pressure-treated cedar shingles
were installed on the restaurant roof and 8,000
square feet of white cedar siding on the exterior.
Hot-fluid-applied roofing was installed over the
kitchen. Maizel Construction was the contractor.**

PERAZICH PROPERTY (1889-1892)

1701 Q Street NW. The brick-and-brownstone residence was designed by Thomas Franklin Schneider in the Romanesque style. Wagner installed new built-in copper gutter and restored Vermont slate roof on the towers and the mansard.

NATIONAL INTREPID CENTER OF EXCELLENCE (NICOE) (2010)

4860 S. Palmer Road, Bethesda, Maryland. The center is an advanced facility dedicated to research, diagnosis and treatment of military personnel and veterans suffering from traumatic brain injury and psychological health issues. The center was officially turned over to the Department of Defense in a ceremony on June 24, 2010. The facility was built with $65 million donated to the Fallen Heroes Fund started by Arnold Fisher. Contractor contributions helped to complete the project ahead of schedule and under budget. The general contractor was Turner Construction; Smith Group was the designer. Wagner installed a 20-year LEED-certified roof and stainless-steel flashings.

Archive photo, circa 1921, via the Library of Congress.

THE ARGYLE (1913)

Architect: Alexander H. Sonnermann. 17th Street and Park Road NW. The building featured costly detailing to appeal to upper middle class Washingtonians of the day. Almost all of the forty apartments had at least one bay window, many with sweeping views of the city and Rock Creek Park. The lobby, main stairway, and corridors were trimmed with expensive snow-white Colorado Yule marble, the same marble used for the Lincoln Memorial and the Tomb of the Unknown Soldier. Monthly rent on a three-bedroom apartment was $28.50. Five-bedroom units went for $32.50. The overhang was rebuilt, and masonry restored to accept 700 linear feet of shop-fabricated lead-coated copper cornice which included the installation of 375 stamped medallions. At upper left, finished cornices with paint. At left, cornices being installed.

Residential

PRIVATE RESIDENCE (1927)
#1 Western red cedar shingles were steamed and bent to fit the rounded corners and the convex portions at the end of the mansard. New copper gutters and downspouts were installed.

PROSPECT HOUSE, LINGAN TEMPLE HOUSE (1788)

3508 Prospect Street NW. It was built by James Lingan and designed by William Thornton, Architect of the Capitol. President John Adams visited the residence and Gilbert du Motier, Marquis de Lafayette, was a house guest. It was a guest house while Blair House was under renovation. New Buckingham slate, copper and rubber roofs, and copper gutters and downspouts were installed. At top left, Randy Herald installs copper finial on the gazebo. Wagner replaced and repainted all the windows and trim.

Before

After

KOGOD RESIDENCE (1918), ABOVE
Also known as the Maie H. Williams House was designed by Clarke Waggaman in a Late Georgian style. Waggaman studied law at Georgetown and Catholic universities and was never formally trained as an architect. Major structural repairs were made, new slate, and lead-coated copper built-in gutters were installed. Above, architect George Hartman, left, approves the slate mockup.

🏛 **LOSCH RESIDENCE (1911), AT RIGHT**
1716 New Hampshire Avenue NW. Wagner repointed the masonry façade, painted all windows and trim and replaced the slate mansard and copper water table.

🏛 MONTEVIDEO (1828-30)

16801 River Road, Seneca, Maryland. It was built in the Federal style by John Parke Custis Peter, with architecture inspired by Tudor Place (designed by William Thornton in 1815), the Georgetown home where Peter grew up. Peter was the son of Thomas Peter and Martha Parke Custis Peter, Martha Washington's granddaughter. Built of Seneca red sandstone (covered in stucco) from Peter's nearby quarry and cutting mill, which also supplied the stone for the Smithsonian Castle and hundreds of buildings around the Washington, D.C., area. Montevideo was restored by Austin and Gogo Kiplinger in 1958 and is now owned by their son Knight Kiplinger. Roof work consisted of maintenance to the slate roofs, gutters, and chimneys.

🏛 BOSTWICK HOUSE (1746)

3901 48th Street, Bladensburg, Maryland. Christopher Lowndes designed the house in the Adamesque style. The shingle roofs on the kitchen addition and the adjacent barn were replaced, and the chimneys on the main house were rebuilt. The porch roof damaged during the earthquake was rebuilt.

🏛 **LOW RESIDENCE (1907)**
Architects: Harding and Upman. 1827 Park Road NW. This home was built in the Georgian revival style. Wagner replaced the tin roof, lead-coated copper valleys and cornice, and installed a copper roof. Residents, Rob and Linda Low are active in preserving Washington history. Photo by Rob Low.

🏛 **WOODWARD HOME (1868)**
The house built by architects Stark, Weather, and Plowman in the Italianate style is on Cookes Row in Georgetown. According to legend, Henry David Cooke built Cookes Row to establish residences for his four children. Wagner installed new Buckingham slate, copper roofing and built-in gutters. Carl Petty was the general contractor.

Beyond
Washington

ST. GEORGE UNIVERSITY, PRESIDENT'S RESIDENCE, GRENADA, WEST INDIES, AT UPPER LEFT
Built structure and covered with copper. Shipped cupola to Grenada and installed using a crane.

McMAHON RESIDENCE, DEEP CREEK LAKE, MARYLAND, AT UPPER RIGHT
Designed and built by John McMahon. Installed standing seam copper roofing.

FEDERAL EMERGENCY MANAGEMENT AGENCY (FEMA), AT RIGHT
16825 S. Seton Avenue, Emmitsburg, Maryland. Replaced 18,000 square feet of slate, and installed copper roofing, gutters and downspouts. General contractor: Wycliffe Enterprises.

ST. PHILIP'S EPISCOPAL CHURCH, LEFT AND CHAPEL, ABOVE
Wagner replaced the Chapel tin roof blown off by Hurricane Hugo in 1989. Architect: Joseph Hyde, the church building (1835-1836) and Edward Brickell White, the steeple (1848-1850). 146 Church Street, Charleston, South Carolina. Photo at left via wikipedia.com.

Material Matters

1808 New Hampshire Avenue NW. Built by Walter Paris, an architect and artist, the building reflects a combination of the Queen Anne and Richardsonian romanesque architectural styles. Wagner made structural and slate repairs, and installed new copper valleys.

At left, the Spanish tile roof in the foreground and the standing-seam copper turret on the Car Barn. In the middle distance, a red tin roof in need of paint on top of 1789 Restaurant. In the background, the slate roof of Georgetown University's Healy Hall.

Above, an original patinaed copper crest, at left, from the DAR Constitution Hall and new stamped copper crest, at right.

Copper's lasting appeal

Copper is elegant, beautiful, and long-lasting. "I used to tell customers, 'You can use tin'" — an age-old medium, much of which is actually 60 percent tin and close to 40 percent lead, Chuck Wagner says. "But by the second time we paint it, you will have spent what you would have spent on copper."

Shiny, salmon-pink copper routinely turns green — or "patinae" — in the atmosphere after a time that differs wildly from city to city, even neighborhood to neighborhood, depending on such factors as the amount of moisture, salt, and sulfur in the air. Acid rain is no friend to copper, either. Copper reacts to harsh elements in stages through oxidation, which forms copper sulfate that turns stages of brown, then almost black, and finally the greenish patinae. Photographs of the Library of Congress's Jefferson Building dome, for instance, show all of these stages over the years. "If the copper is on a building on the seacoast, the green patina will emerge in just a few years," H. Wayne Seale, a now-retired Copper Development Association official, notes. "If it's in Las Vegas, you'll never have green copper; it will remain brown forever."

The copper in each case had "reached its weathering equilibrium," Seale adds. "That's what gives copper its long life."

Some copper doesn't turn green because its trace elements have been removed. Or it has been coated in lead because it's going to come into contact with zinc or galvanized iron that could potentially cause electrolysis — the passage of electric current across a roof.

Uniqueness of slate

Slate — natural, delicate, and beautiful — is the material for which Wagner Roofing is renowned. "Of course, money is a factor" in choosing a roofing material, Chuck Wagner told The Washington Post in 2002. And the expense of slate has to be considered.

But, Wagner added, "usually the person who selects slate lives in a traditional neighborhood" where slate roofs are admired and treasured. "These homeowners are purists, and it's the character of the neighborhood and the house that they want to maintain."

Local builder Jim Gibson, who has hired Wagner Roofing to complete a number of slate-roof jobs, told The Post, "People are spending a fair amount of money to make their house look old and authentic," and slate fits their style.

Slate is mined from a number of quarries: bluish slate from nearby Virginia and multicolored slate from Vermont. It is machine-cut into huge blocks, reduced further using jackhammers, and sliced yet again by diamond blades.

Varying sizes of slate can be important for perspective.

Smaller is better on a small roof, and tapering of sizes on certain roofs is pleasing to the eye.

At the quarry, each slate has two holes punched for copper nails — an update on the hand-whittled wooden pegs that once did the job — that will affix them to a roof. If a slate must be cut to fit — much as one often needs to cut a row of floor tiles to make them exactly fit a room — it's the slater on site who uses a special hammer to do it. That hammer has a place for cutting slate,

Above, tools used by sheet metal workers.

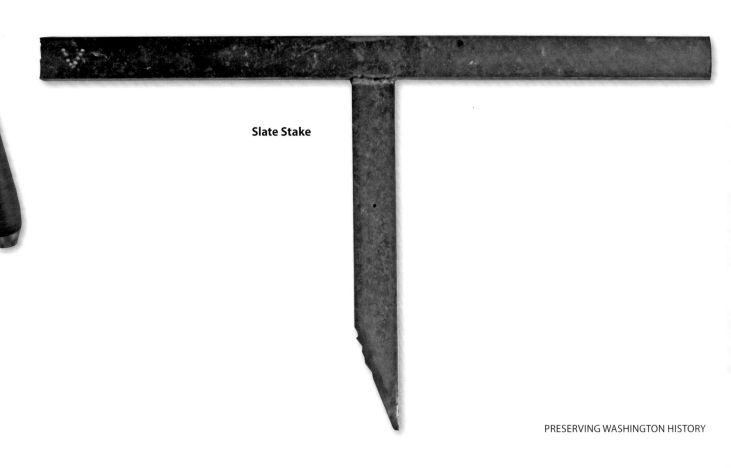

Slate Hammer

Slate Stake

pulling nails, and a sharp end for punching nail holes in the newly cut piece.

When slate is applied, in "courses" that overlap sufficiently to keep out the rain, the classic look is that of, in Jack Wagner Jr.'s words, "a fine museum in the sky."

Expert slaters use the "ping" test to judge a slate shingle's quality. Struck with a flicked finger, quality slate will ring like a bell. And fine slate lasts relatively forever. One slate company in Buckingham, Virginia, guarantees its slate shingles for the life of a building. The slate at Yale University is holding tight, without a hint of discoloration, more than 200 years after it was nailed to dozens of buildings.

The puzzle presented by slate occurs when a slate roof is damaged and replacement shingles must be found. Even though the roof may be viewed from afar, finding close matches in color and striation is a satisfying adventure.

How tile stacks up

Wagner Roofing has put on many wood-shingle and terra-cotta tile roofs.

The former sometimes requires that shingles be steamed and bent to fit around turrets and domes, and the latter presents a problem of recent vintage: For reasons no one has satisfactorily explained, some manufacturers of terra-cotta have hardened their tiles to the point that mechanics wear out even carbon-steel drill bits working with them. "Only the underlayment and flashings deteriorate over time," Chuck Wagner says, "and those can be replaced." He recommends annual checks, though, for broken tiles caused by painters, gutter cleaners, and others who may what walked on the roof.

"Keep the fiddlers off the roof," he advises.

SHAND RESIDENCE
Vermont Avenue and T Street NW. After a fire that destroyed this 1878 house, Wagner used photographs and a video to replicate a hand-cut slate roof that matched its original beauty.

2013
NRCA
GOLD CIRCLE
AWARD

Presented to
Wagner
Roofing Co.

2013
NRCA
GOLD CIRCLE
AWARD

Awards & Accolades

Trophy case: 2013 awards from the National Roofing Contractors Association, received for Outstanding Workmanship and Innovative Solutions on the U.S. Naval Academy's Mahan Hall, flank the the award for Best Overall Project of the year.

2012
1st Place Subcontractor Appreciation Award

2010
6th & I Synagogue — Restoration/Renovation under $100 million

2006
Kreeger Museum — Restoration/Renovation under $100 million

2005
Robert F. Kennedy Main Justice Building — Marvin Black Excellence in Partnering Award

2004
Robert F. Kennedy Main Justice Building — Subcontractor of the Year

Associated Builders and Contractors, Inc.

1993
Franklin School
— Outstanding Craftsmanship

2013
Capitol Hill Seventh Day Adventist Church
— Feature Article

U.S. Naval Academy's Mahan Hall
— Feature Article

2011
6th & I Synagogue — Feature Article

2006
Kreeger Museum — Feature Article

2005
Robert F. Kennedy Main Justice Building
— Feature Article

KETTLER BROTHERS

1959
Commercial Subcontractor of the Year

SMITHSONIAN FOLKLIFE FESTIVAL

2001
Presentation of Slate and Sheet Metal Craftsmanship at the Smithsonian Center for Folklife and Cultural Heritage

American Institute of Architecture

1992
Franklin School — Award for Excellence

GILBANE

2004
Robert F. Kennedy Main Justice Building
— Recognition of Excellence in Performance

2013
Outstanding Workmanship
Steep-slope

Wagner Roofing Co.

Hyattsville, Md.

for U.S. Naval Academy's Mahan Hall

Annapolis, Md.

NRCA
Gold Circle Awards

2013
U. S. Naval Academy — Gold Circle Awards for Outstanding Workmanship and Innovative Solutions; and Platinum Award for Best Overall Project

2009
Dan Williams — Most Valuable Player Award

2005
Robert F. Kennedy Main Justice Building — Gold Circle Award for Outstanding Workmanship

2001
Bob Wooldridge — Most Valuable Player

Participation in the Pentagon Roof Project

163

CRAFTSMANSHIP AWARD

THIS IS TO CERTIFY THAT

J. S. WAGNER CO. INC.

EMPLOYER

IS HEREBY PRESENTED WITH THIS AWARD BY
THE BUILDING CONGRESS AND EXCHANGE OF METROPOLITAN BALTIMORE, INC.
IN RECOGNITION OF EXCEPTIONAL CRAFTSMANSHIP SHOWN IN THE

REMOVAL AND RE-INSTALLATION
OF THE DECORATIVE PATTERN SLATE ROOF

AT

GALLAGHER MANSION SENIOR HOUSING
BALTIMORE, MARYLAND

1997

BOB WOOLDRIDGE
CRAFTSMAN

HARKINS BUILDERS, INC.
GENERAL CONTRACTOR

GOVANS ECUMENICAL
DEVELOPMENT CORPORATION
OWNER

SMEALLIE, ORRICK AND JANKA, LTD.
ARCHITECT

N. Frederick Churchman
PRESIDENT, BUILDING CONGRESS & EXCHANGE

CHAIRMAN, CRAFTSMANSHIP AWARDS COMMITTEE

Building Congress & Exchange

1997
Gallagher Mansion — Craftsmanship Award

AGC of Metropolitan Washington D.C.
congratulates

Wagner Roofing

for their participation on
Military Advanced Training Center at Walter Reed Hospital
for
Turner Construction Company
2007 Washington Contractor Merit Award
New Construction

164

ARMED FORCES AMPUTEE
PATIENT CARE PROGRAM

This certificate is to acknowledge

WAGNER ROOFING

for their mission accomplishment on the
Military Amputee Training Center project for
Wounded Warriors at
Walter Reed Army Medical Center

Charles R. Scoville

CHARLES R. SCOVILLE, PROGRAM MANAGER

13 APRIL 2007

DAVIS BUCKLEY A PROFESSIONAL CORPORATION

ARCHITECTS AND PLANNING CONSULTANTS, SIXTEEN TWELVE K STREET, NORTHWEST, SUITE 900, WASHINGTON, D.C., 20006 (202) 223-1234 FAX (202) 223-1212

May 17, 2007

Mr. Chuck Wagner, President
Wagner Roofing
4909 46th Avenue
Hyattsville, MD 20781

Project: Woodlawn ~ Conservation and Restoration of the Exterior Envelope
            Stage 1: Roofing, Gutters, Wood Trim and Porch Restoration

Dear Mr. Wagner;

I wanted to take this opportunity to express how pleased Davis Buckley Architects and Planners is with the work that your company recently completed at Woodlawn, in Mt. Vernon, Virginia. This national landmark structure, completed in 1805 on a tract of land broken off from his estate by George Washington, and designed by William Thornton, the first architect of the US Capitol, required nothing less than the highest level of care.

In your role as general contractor and roofing contractor, Wagner Roofing performed professionally, efficiently and creatively on this technically challenging assignment. Bob Coberly, Wagner Roofing's project manager, did an excellent job managing the schedule, Wagner's subcontractors, and a busy site that remained open to the public throughout construction. Bob acted quickly and productively to remedy any unforseen, concealed conditions that were occasionally uncovered during the course of the project.

Wagner's roofing foreman, Bob Wooldridge, and his crew demonstrated the highest level of craftsmanship and technical expertise throughout the installation of the new slate roof on an existing substrate that often varied its construction and dimensions, from one area to the next.

We were please when the National Trust for Historic Preservation first selected Wagner Roofing as the general contractor for this important project, and remain so today at its completion. Congratulations on a job well done.

Sincerely,

Thomas J. Striegel

Thomas J. Striegel, AIA, LEED AP
Vice President
Project Manager for the Woodlawn Conservation and Restoration

Chuck

Once again I say:
Your "Rooflines"
is the best publication
of its kind I have ever
seen. I not only
read it. I relish it!
Thanks,
and
Merry Christmas

Austin Kiplinger

12/22/08

WAGNER ROOFLINES

Wagner Roofing
100 Years

Since 1914

WINTER 2014

Wagner Roofing Company • Roofing & Sheet Metal Contractors Since 1914 • 301/927/9030 • wagnerroofing.com

Legendary DC Mansion Celebrates Centennial and New Roof

When Wagner Roofing began working on the roof at the Washington International School, no one expected to find an anniversary gift atop the historic mansion. But that's exactly what the Wagner crew dug up, in the form of a century-old slate. The slate was engraved with "Aug. 1913" and the initials "F.B.," likely the name of the engraver. So in 2013, the slate was removed from the roof, and in the fall, it was bequeathed to the Washington International School to celebrate the 100th anniversary of its home.

Set on a hill and surrounded by trees in Cleveland Park, the Washington International School took up residence on the estate in 1972. But the century-old mansion recorded a rich history long before any students arrived.

Designed by architect Charles Platt – the only residence he ever designed in Washington– the Beaux Art country house sits in the middle of an estate that includes a large formal garden, a gardener's cottage, a carriage house, informal gardens and hundreds of ornamental trees. There are a couple of streams, a pond, arches, fountains and walkways.

The original owners of the estate were James and Alice Parmelee, whose interests included travel and art collection. A businessman who was also vice president of the Corcoran, James was one of the largest donors to the National Cathedral building project; Alice was involved in planning the gardens on the grounds of the Cathedral. (Three stained-glass windows from their home are now on display at the Cathedral.)

The next owners of the house were Ambassador Joseph Davies and Marjorie Merriweather Post, of the Post cereal family. They renamed the estate Tregaron and lived there from 1942 until the mid-50s, when the couple separated. Merriweather Post entertained extensively, and there was even a nine-hole "pitch and putt" golf course on the estate, with little Tregaron scorecards; President Eisenhower is said to have enjoyed golfing there.

Dorothy Goodman's Washington International School signed its first lease on the property in 1972. In

**The Mansion, 1914-2014
Celebrates 100 years**

1980, the school purchased the 10 acres that include all the estate's buildings. Today, the former servants quarters are administrative offices; the kitchen and laundry are classrooms and office spaces; and the drawing room is a media center and library. The estate was designated under the National Register of Historic Places in 1990.

When the school began searching for a roofing company to repair the roof of the mansion, other private schools in Washington suggested Wagner. "Wagner

continued on page 3

CELEBRATING Wagner Roofing 100 Years

1

Wagner Roofing
100 Years
Since 1914

4909 46th Avenue
Hyattsville, Maryland 20781

wagnerroofing.com

telephone: (301) 927-9030
fax: (301) 927-3505

Photo by Chris Zarconi. zarconiphoto.com

Preserving Washington History

100 YEARS *of* WAGNER ARTISTRY

Through partnerships with our loyal customers, we find our most fulfilling work: preserving our buildings for future generations.

Please contact us at
info@preservingwashingtonhistory.com

— Chuck and Sheila Wagner